I AM I

The Indweller of Your Heart

BOOK ONE

Also by David Knight

Pathway

Deliverance of Love, Light and Truth

I am I: The Indweller of Your Heart—Book Two

I am I: The Indweller of Your Heart—Book Three

I am I: The Indweller of Your Heart—'Collection'

Leave the Body Behind—Sojourns of the Soul

A Pocket Full of God

I AM I

The Indweller of Your Heart

BOOK ONE

52 LESSONS TO HELP YOU OVERCOME THE EMOTIONAL WATERS OF LIFE

David Knight

I AM I The Indweller of Your Heart—Book One

Copyright © 2011 & © 2016 by DPK Publishing–AscensionForYou.

Previous ISBN–13: 978-1-4664993-5-5
This edition–ISBN: 978-1-8380091-6-8
    eISBN: 978-1-914936-03-6

Updated Version Copyright © 2021 DPK Publishing–AscensionForYou.
Printed in the United States of America.

All rights reserved and the moral right of the Author has been asserted. Without limiting the rights under copyright reserved above, no part of this publication may be reproduced, stored in or introduced into a retrieval system, or transmitted, in any form, or by any means (electronic, mechanical, photocopying, recording, or otherwise) without the prior written permission of both the copyright owner and the above publisher of this book.

A CIP catalogue record for this book is available from the British library.

2021 Cover layout/design by Nathan Dasco

For further information contact David via his website/blog:
https://www.AscensionForYou.com

If you enjoy reading *I AM I The Indweller of Your Heart—Book One*, you can find further inspiring and motivation books when you join David's mission for a 'full and blissful life'.

To learn more, visit www.AscensionForYou.com and download ***Deliverance of Love, Light and Truth*** for free.

ACKNOWLEDGMENTS

To God, for the privilege that has been bestowed upon me so that I may receive these words of wisdom, knowledge, and peace. This book has created a new steppingstone towards the eternal love and bliss that is within us all.

To all my guides and teachers from within God's light hierarchy who have truly given and shared their love so freely, making my life—and heart—so rich and complete, that mere words cannot begin to describe how I feel.

I wish to thank my wife Caroline in recognition of her support, patience, and love. To Adeline Teh (Sai Divine Inspirations), Robert Paskin, Elizabeth Beeton and Joleene Naylor, Rachael Hardcastle and Nathan Dasco for all their support, advice, and time! To all members, past and present, of the Peterborough Sai Baba group and finally, thank you to my family and friends, who are all so special to me.

MAY GOD BLESS YOU ALL

TABLE OF CONTENTS

FOREWORD..15

INTRODUCTION FROM ARCHANGEL GABRIEL 17

JESUS ... The Lord Our 'Teacher' (With guidance and love to you all)..19

LESSON 1: I AM THAT I AM....................................22

LESSON 2: THE 'INDWELLER' OF THE HEART.................24

LESSON 3: WHO AM I?...26

LESSON 4: RITUALS AND MONUMENTS............................29

LESSON 5: POWER OF LOVE.....................................32

LESSON 6: STILLNESS...34

LESSON 7: ENERGY..37

LESSON 8: GRIEF, 'HEART-ACHE' AND THEN JOY...........39

LESSON 9: JOY OUT OF DARKNESS.............................42

LESSON 10: THE 'GOAL'...45

LESSON 11: THREE..48

LESSON 12: A CHRISTMAS CAROL......................................51

LESSON 13: PEACE AND GOODWILL..................................54

LESSON 14: STAR OF WONDER...57

LESSON 15: MISSING YOU..60

LESSON 16: ACCEPTANCE...63

LESSON 17: EXPRESSION..66

LESSON 18: CREATIVITY LEADS TO FREEDOM AND EXPRESSION...69

LESSON 19: FREEDOM AND POWER...................................72

LESSON 20: INFINITY 75

LESSON 21: THOUGHTS..78

LESSON 22: COMPASSION 81

LESSON 23: DEEDS NOT WORDS...84

LESSON 24: 'TRUST AND FAITH'..87

LESSON 25: TRUST IN YOU AND ME 90

LESSON 26: FROM 'CHILDHOOD' TO 'ADULTHOOD' 93

LESSON 27: SIGNPOSTS 96

LESSON 28: THE 'LESSON' 99

LESSON 29: 1000 ('I's) 101

LESSON 30: ENLIGHTENMENT 103

LESSON 31: UNITED 107

LESSON 32: HEAVEN 110

LESSON 33: MIRACLES 113

LESSON 34: FEELINGS 116

LESSON 35: PERSEVERANCE 119

LESSON 36: 'APPRECIATION' 122

LESSON 37: RESPONSIBILITY 125

LESSON 38: MERCY 128

LESSON 39: SPIRITUAL EDUCATION AND MEMORY 131

LESSON 40: FAMILY AND THE TREE OF LIFE 134

LESSON 41: OASIS 137

LESSON 42: DREAMS AND VISIONS 140

LESSON 43: MYSTERIES 143

LESSON 44: NATURE 146

LESSON 45: BEING 'STILL' IN A WEB OF LIFE 149

LESSON 46: EACH A 'SUN' – WITH FREE WILL 151

LESSON 47: LIGHT AND SIGHT TO NEW LEVELS 154

LESSON 48: PARALLEL LINES 157

LESSON 49: GUILT … OR SHAME? 160

LESSON 50: WAR AND PEACE, LOVE AND HATE 163

LESSON 51: HAPPINESS 166

LESSON 52: THE CHOICE 169

CONCLUSION—Part 1: 'GOD'S LOVE' 177

CONCLUSION—Part 2: 'GO IN PEACE AND WITH

FORGIVENESS' 174

FURTHER READING 176

ABOUT THE AUTHOR..178

INVITATION FROM DAVID KNIGHT....................................179

FOREWORD

Welcome my son. Much time in your world has passed—and yet, in reality, no time at all.

Over the years … since the collation of Book 2—Deliverance of Love, Light, and Truth, we have watched and waited while your busy life unfolded. Through many trials and tribulations, both joy and happiness have prevailed. Love and Light will always shine strongly from within your heart and far beyond the four walls in which you live.

Your understanding of whom, what, and why you exist has grown considerably over the first two books. Thoughts and feelings have frequently emanated from your mind's eye—and heart—regarding the subject and content for this new 'work'. Therefore, it is now time David for you to collate and contribute to another book.

Since your spirituality has given you new insights—growing brighter and lighter over time—you have realised beyond doubt we are all 'whole'. One's shape or form, and levels of intellect of a being, bear no resemblance to the love that is carried within, and which is given so freely.

People say beauty is in the 'eye' of the beholder and yet genuine beauty comes from the source of all things. This is God, the creator, the Great White Spirit, or whichever name or form an individual agrees within himself what pure love is.

Through the education of your soul—in this lifetime—you have progressed and come a long way, my son. And yet ... you have been nowhere else in time or space ... other than the moment that exists within each second, minute, hour, day, week, or year.

There is no separation from truth and the light. For all your experiences, the happiest of all is within the 'stillness' and the bliss of love itself. So, we ask those who have picked up this new (and your third) book: where is this truth, peace, and tranquillity? Well, it is in the greatest power and the brightest light and the most beautiful sight and sound inside you. This is your essence, and the very core of your existence!

Deep within your soul and heart is the love you all seek and cherish so dearly. There is no need to travel over mountains or hide away in forests to find the answers to all things. God is everything and everything is God. He/she dwells as the fountain of joy, cascading tears of love and peace to all who come to bathe in him.

I AM I The Indweller of Your Heart—Book One

'I am I: The Indweller of Your Heart' is to be the title of this latest work, David. You will hear, speak, and confide in the creator, so more people comprehend and accept their own reality. Information and dictation of words will flow similarly to what we have accustomed to you.

Others may consider that you—or we—are mad, whilst others might decree that you are indeed privileged. Your faith, hope and character have all helped in being where you are today. Always listen to your heart and you will discover and hear the truth.

God provides the correct timing for the written word, for the benefit of society and humanity. All words and truth are simple and will be simply put. Doctrines and beliefs of many religions can often be complex, but 'love and truth' is not, and spiritual education is not either.

The content will amaze you. Some passages will make you cry with tears of peace and love. Others will make you feel that deep inside your heart there is light, glowing so brightly that people will see and feel the same within themselves, too.

David, it is so good to reconnect your pen with our hearts. We entwine our lives. Your thoughts, wishes and your dreams are also felt by us too. Your earthbound time may seem to pass by quickly, but we have always been close, waiting patiently for you. We love you. We love you all.

Remember, the stars and planets above and beyond where we physically live may seem an eternity away, but the mind's perception only tries to deceive. Space, the universe and time itself are but a minute fragment, not even the size of an atom on the Lord's foot. People want to think 'outside the box', but there is no box. Just experience the truth within.

May those who seek to inquire about reality—the aspirant or devotee—and the disciples of different races, religions, and any being; understand we are but one family of love. Connected are we all by the true source of illumination and power—the one 'light' and one truth—the 'Indweller' of all our hearts.

So, collate the written words for this new book—the tug of the heartstrings will guide you with the timing. God's love and words will flow Just be still and be you. Live, breathe, know, and experience it.

For now, be at peace. Know that many souls had drawn close, and now wave goodbye. They wait patiently for your tasks ahead. When it is necessary and appropriate, we will reconnect our own 'pen' to the energy inside you. From love and light within, across time, space, and dimensions ... good luck, my son.

INTRODUCTION FROM ARCHANGEL GABRIEL

You sit as a young child, yet you are not. Appearances for many are such an important thing and the phrase, 'Beauty is only skin deep' is, of course, well known to you all.

Sitting eagerly to grow and patiently to know, the stillness will sustain and nourish everyone, in more ways than you can imagine. It is a replenishment of the soul, just as a deep sleep re-energises aching limbs and muscles of the 'physical'.

Spirit works through you and is you; you are spirit ... and yet why question the need for sustenance? A simple lesson would be to think of a battery cell. When used, it will expel and radiate energy and, as a soul/cell of the universal life force, you are no different.

Do not envisage that God would cut you off from the power supply, for you cannot be. And yet, by avoidance of the genuine connection of yourself (both positive and negative), you then—as you have heard this very afternoon—become unbalanced. How and why is this so? Who decrees it and for what purpose? What motives lie hidden?

Nothing, dear child, hides. The mind's perception cannot see the truth unless true sight is born from within oneself and thy heart, which is your seat of the soul. You see me sitting within you, opposite you and deep within your psyche, yet am I not as real as your body?

People wish to learn and digest, but they can place too much on the emphasis of their own natural senses. Although these are important, one can neglect the sixth sense ... your intuition or 'gut-feelings' and what you feel is right from 'within'.

So, I am here, and you are too. Where I am and where I go, you are with me. In the spirit realms and dimensions, distance and time have no meaning. You are spirit and I am spirit too, and levels of understanding and growth, knowledge and wisdom, time, space, and dimensions are all linked as 'one' since time immemorial.

God is love; love is God. Light is God, God is light. Spirit is God, God is spirit, and nothing is divisible or subtracted from your core essence. Your power (light) can only diminish if you place a cloak of darkness around it yourselves. Your karma and your balance will always be yours to attain, and to cleanse and polish your 'living' flame.

Obscurity of the soul and your memories can only be a last resort after many trials and tribulations of countless lifetimes have not developed the 'inner' you. This is an individual soul's choice because you are a seed of love left to grow, but never left alone, as you well know.

Through thick and thin, your efforts to expand your love will never be in vain. Your desire to learn even expands your energy, which is fascinating to observe. Positive thought creates spirals of light and truth that radiate infinitely long, but I can say the same of darkness and decay. So, the calmness of soul and body and mind must be one to 'become'.

Know that light travels in all directions and also follows the same paths in reverse to your thoughts. Therefore, you can comprehend, "So you give and so you shall receive" and also, "So you sow, so shall you reap."

> Light expands Light,
> Love expands Love,
> Desire expands the fire.
> The flame expands God's name,
> The name expands the 'grain',
> The 'grain' expands the same,
> The same holds no blame.
> Now blame can hold disdain,
> And disdain keeps the shame,
> For shame can lead to blame.
> The circles round again,
> And 'one' you shall remain.
> Until light has led the way,
> It's eternal and a day.
>
> (Now realise)
>
> A shining star is both far and near,
> So, search within and do not fear.
> It radiates with love and light,
> And we entwine our hearts all day and night.
>
> Know that rose-coloured glasses or blurred vision,
> Can erase or fade your soul's true mission.
> That you and 'all' exist to grow,
> To ascend the cord that you will sow.
> Amen

JESUS ... The Lord Our 'Teacher'
(With guidance and love to you all).

Welcome dear 'children' of love and light, that's it, sit down. I receive all here for truth, love, and liberty.

Know that our hearts are like the many rooms of an immeasurable house, my Father's House. If you can imagine an exceptionally large mansion, you may think that you would forget some of these rooms, wouldn't you? But he doesn't, for he knows where each of his children reside, every minute of the day.

You might get lost or confused inside such a large place with all these different rooms, levels, and floors of life. You learn and you yearn both for knowledge and wisdom, yet these must come from your own experiences. Patience little ones, for as some of you know, you cannot learn any more than the level that you have reached.

Trust in love and love the trust that my father has instilled in each one of you. Open your physical eyes, and those of your mind, soul, and heart, too. Only then do you get true vision. Yes, seen more clearly, felt more dearly, and understood with true love. No guilt, no pretence, and no sitting on the proverbial fence.

You gather here because of love and the sharing of such far beyond these four walls. No box can contain or hide what I reveal and is free to flow to where it is meant to go. I entwined hearts like the ivy that wraps around the tree. The ivy clings to the tree and wants to climb to the top, to reach the light. Likewise, you also wish to climb and also reach out to the 'tree of life' that is around and yet also within you too.

The bark of the tree enables you to grip and stay in place, so the light can reflect and radiate from within and from your face. A smile (yes, that's right), so be happy, for you are all from the seed and an eternal 'trace can reveal this'.

Time can be so important, yet it can mean nothing at all. Thousands of tomorrows, no need to beg, steal or borrow. You are all given what you need and required to experience physically, spiritually, emotionally, and mentally. Some things are, of course, your own tests; while others are for what you can do for your fellow 'hearts' along the way. Balance is the key, and your love is the door, to be opened and enable you to search for more.

I AM I The Indweller of Your Heart—Book One

Do not worry or concern yourselves where each of you comes from, for no matter how different you all appear to be, you are the same, yes, all the same to your 'Father' and to me. Precious, like flowers and the drops of the rain ... which bring sustenance and nourishment and never in vain. You'll glow and radiate and spiral around, for love, true love, it knows no bounds.

You'll also reach out and search both far and wide, overseas and across the land, and you'll look to the sky. Sometimes there'll be pain and sometimes there'll be joy and the gift of a new-born child is indeed not a toy. With a chance to fulfil—and to also instil—to find the love from above, taking flight like a dove.

Angels and archangels in Heaven and on Earth both look and assist the meek and the mirth. Some are below and some are above, all with their 'work' from the Lord and our God. To aid and assist you in all that you do, be glad, be safe, for He and I are in you. Go north, south, east, and west ... just try to do all, with love and your best. And so...

>Different rooms of the house, but hearts are all safe,
>For God has enveloped and surrounded you with a 'fate'.
>For you are all 'from' and return unto Him,
>So, rejoice and all sing just like love within a hymn.
>
>You will all grow as I have just said,
>Just try to believe and rise from your bed.
>Whether morning or noon or evening or night,
>The days that you walk will remain always bright.
>
>The golden 'Son' forever glows, deep within your hearts,
>Can never be extinguished or be divided into parts.
>For each segment, each band, and vibration or sound,
>Is eternal and, as stated, true love knows no bounds.
>
>Each day is a link, and the chain keeps you all,
>No 'separation and division', or an 'unearthly' fall.
>So even if your life then hits a new low,
>Call unto your 'Father', for he already knows.
>
>Of what you require and of what you would all like,
>To happen and 'emerge', yes from 'within' and out life.
>Just 'be' and to ask with all of your heart,
>For the Lord knows, too, of what's right from the start.

I AM I The Indweller of Your Heart—Book One

The teacher is no man or with a false text,
It is the light and the love that is 'within' that's the test.
So, justify the why and then hear the call,
To know then, dear 'children', you can never, ever fall.

Just be 'still'; be still … for you are the 'divine',
And you are all 'one'… and each is all mine.
Not a possession cast aside or washed up by the tide,
For the crown of my heart, I give freely, openly, and I will never, ever hide.

Amen.

LESSON 1:

I AM THAT I AM

I welcome you all ... so why ask me—as if to seek permission—to come into my home and kingdom? Know that when you expand and radiate the love within your heart, you will understand you are actually here! No separation or division exists, and while many forms of life may deem you as my 'children'; you are all eternally part of me. In addition, comprehend that inside you is the essence of what you already give, share, and search for too.

Love is infinite, and no dimension of time, space or any plane of consciousness can ever distract from this, for I am all things and, of course, so much more. Believe you are too, as you are me and I am you. We are not apart ... or a 'part' of anything else, for all are 'one' and fulfil Creation.

Do not fear, stress, or worry if you struggle to comprehend this, because learning is constant and forever, so do not feel pressured or think you are running out of time. In fact, what you discover always materialises at the right moment and place, even though you sometimes seem held back or may become frustrated.

Realise too, many virtues and various traits lie deep within you all ... but every fibre, cell, and particle, which forms your being, is the same. You are each unique and, as I will always reiterate, you are still 'one'. Indeed, you may be diverse—in size, height, and character—and capable of different emotions and feelings, but the truth of you has no differences at all!

Since time immemorial and across billions of worlds, many forms of life pray to me with their questions ... but they only need to turn within themselves to find their answers. Listening to the silence is the easiest way to hear me. Remember, I reside inside your heart—and in every thought and deed—because dear child of light, I AM I.

David, as you write these words, I sense a query flash through your consciousness ... but do not concern yourself if people say these words are formed through a child of God. Some will wonder how this is possible ... for light to pass through the mind and hand to control a pen. Well, this is no mystery or complex issue to discover, manipulate or bend, for you are I and I am you. As such, know and understand...

My love is your love in all that I send,
For everything am I ... be it a Father, Mother or friend.
In every leaf and rock and on land, sea, and air,
You will find truth and the light, for I reside there.

So please trust in your heart whilst learning to care,
Know your heart can be open to both feel and then share.
Within your dreams, wishes and those prayers I do hear,
Cherished laughter and a smile … or those tears I will clear.

For I recognize all hearts, filled with emotions which scar,
Yet in truth lies the door, for my heart is ajar.
Though love taken away may seem to cause pain,
But for those in the 'experience', this is never in vain.

Please realise 'love' cannot fade, like your memories may do,
For the heart retains truth, and the truth is in you.
Therefore, my light and my love are for each and everything,
So open heart, mind, and soul ... to rejoice and now sing.

Then you will know, deep down and inside,
I am in you, and I shall not hide.

Amen.

LESSON 2:

THE 'INDWELLER' OF THE HEART

I am you and you are me, not born or created other than through thought, word, or deed. Therefore, as many of you now seek and desire to grow in truth—both from the inside and out—there comes a time when your own realization takes place. This can occur during your sojourn upon the 'earth-plane', in the realm people call 'Heaven', or upon any of the innumerable dimensions or planes ... because you recognise the reality when it touches the very core of the heart. No amount of persuasion, or any forceful act (via body or tongue), can make someone or something truly 'understand' ... and the self—the true 'self'—realises this.

So, comprehend all life is moving physically, mentally, and emotionally. Amongst this perpetual resonance lays the true stillness, and yet so many people cannot believe this, which resembles a child given a complex sum to do, scratching their head or perhaps even screaming out in frustration ... but one day they will. Therefore, when the individual embarks upon their own road to discovery, they too can become confused, and even walk the 'path of tears' of so many souls, of the past, present, and the future, too.

Perhaps one may consider this point of your life as a test or even the learning curve of the physical embodiment in which you find yourself. Ponder and think about this when you can. For now, try to visualise a flower that blooms within your heart, its petals opening to the rays of light from the Sun. This is the truth of all things, as each petal represents facets of your 'Atma', your soul, your very identity.

The warmth of the Sun clears the way, so the fragrance—which is your divinity—can blossom within you and your surroundings ... as well as in the elements and all creation. Remember, the energy of love and peace and light is pure and cannot become tainted (or misled) by any known or unknown force.

Appreciate that the world's countless scientists and philosophers always search for answers and clues to life in obscure and faraway places. But why look through the darkness when everything you wish to know is already inside you. That said, while they continually strive to discover and venture beyond themselves and the Earth, human endeavour can achieve so much, and within those actions of man, there can be beauty too.

One's goal should be to realise the truth and obtain liberation and bliss ... and ultimately find God, Nirvana, or whatever name a person wishes to call 'me' or 'I'. In fact, everyone must move on from belief systems of bygone eras, such as a 'figurehead', image, or statue, and even beyond a faith or religion, in order to value the legitimacy of our love as 'one'. You can cast this aside as being a joke or farce, or grasp this reality with both hands, for the petals of your heart shall open and those rays of light will prevail, guiding the seeker of truth towards the right path. No matter your age, the ability to comprehend these things remains ... if you really want to.

As such, I 'feel' what you feel, though i your emotions could hurt me, then this would only occur when precious time is wasted. This is not because of your hobbies or through any 'work' you do, but regarding the opportunities which arise in your life to shine like beacons of love. Indeed, circumstances in and around you present many openings for you to share the beauty within each other, but these so often pass you by.

In fact, too much emphasis is upon the material or with selfish acts that blind, trap and twist the cords of truth, which lay before and around all things. I bear witness to these comparisons, as they encompass both the individual and the masses, but you can untangle yourself by letting your love bloom. Try to let these feelings fly upon the wind—just like pollen—knowing that where it falls becomes blessed with my grace and multiplied beyond comprehension.

Please understand love is the nectar of my heart, and I long for each of you to sense its sweet taste and embrace purity once more ... so do not become fooled by the transient and impermanent physical world, as this is an illusion. All you have to do is to turn and look within yourself, and you will discover who and what you really are, and what you can become, too.

I know you all, and there are no secrets which you can keep, and no actions go unfelt—or even unheard—by me, while you are awake or are asleep ... so what you do and think culminates and manifests in karma (action), during your embodiment. I urge you to break free from this cycle of physical renewal, and if you wish, want, and desire it with all that you are and all that you can be, you will become true to your soul and goal.

Consequently, I sense and know you because I am you, the 'Indweller' of your heart. In accepting and understanding this, you become near and dear to me, so comprehend there is absolutely nothing you cannot achieve. Remember, if something is truthful and for love, I make this happen. Every one of you can at least consider or make this decision and choose a reality, but do you believe? I will leave your thoughts on this matter for now. All love, love all ... and you will know and hear my call. Blessed be. Amen.

LESSON 3:
WHO AM I?

Welcome again to the stillness and the peace, away from all the earthly things which trouble your mind and heart. Understand it is here and here alone where your own self-realization can take place ... and this is the only route and direction (which all must take) towards fulfilment and joy.

As I begin this lesson today, many souls gather around you to listen and learn. Spiritual education, or moreover your education of your spirit or soul, does not cease through (or from) birth or death, they are steppingstones to aid you. In fact, through these 'cycles' to erase the radiating coil of darkness and karma, you pass through many lifetimes, and so, deep 'within' is where you choose or determine this path for yourselves. How much a soul or fragment of light grows—and becomes lighter and brighter—is not set in stone, but dependent only upon their own choices.

Please believe you are all aided and guided too, though as I stated once before, 'you can lead a horse to water, but you cannot make it drink'. Do not be annoyed or offended by this statement (as this is not my intention) ... for only through your own endeavours can you understand and therefore grow in knowledge and wisdom.

Remember, I am with you always and forever; you are never alone. By simply acknowledging this, you will believe in me ... and in yourself, too. All your adversities and experiences, and also your joy and happiness, will merge, going hand in hand along your journey to discover and help you realise who I am.

You may well read the last sentence and sense the same expression in the question, 'Who am I?' To the reader and the disciple of love and truth, they can seem quite different, but they are not. This is because the 'who I am and who am I?' questions are but a reflection of one truth, the inner reality, the secret, the desire, and the goal for all souls. Therefore, you are me and I am you ... the 'I am that I am' or God in me 'IS'.

These are two of the countless expressions which try to convey and represent me in words. This is impossible ... because I am the formless 'form' and the nameless 'name'. Only by finding the truth within will you find me ... and only then can you understand the truth and be able to answer the question in the title of this lesson. One may now ask, "Is this easy?"

Well, to begin with, you must first find reconciliation with yourself, not by trying to change or even thinking you can alter the past, but in the way you view how the past 'was.'

Those negative traits or energies need to fade from your heart. This is vital in order to move forward into love and light ... so let them go. Do not become restrained—or limited—by sorrow, grief, heartache, or attachment to any situation, event, or by people who come into (or go out of) your life. Then, by trusting in this fluidity, everything you experience becomes an element of growth as both a human being and a soul. This will encourage and enable you to keep an unbiased viewpoint of your living in the present ...., erasing the trickery of the mind, which tries to enforce your notion of something being 'good or bad' within your experiences'.

Remember, for the present to become a form of magical living, you need to open your heart towards the richness of peace and serenity through the energy of love living throughout creation. Ultimately, you are your own teacher, educator, principal, and source of divine inspiration and guidance, but should one discard this idea, the answer becomes unknowable, even if right in front of you.

Therefore, I do not hide from your view, inside a secret cave within a distant nation. I am not residing upon a faraway shoreline you cannot reach ... or even lie behind a veil of stars in the night sky. Likewise, I am not above you in a make-believe Heaven, sitting upon a golden throne. I am not below you ... holding the earth aloft upon my shoulders, either.

What I am 'is' who I am, and who am I is what I am.
This is no riddle or joke to confuse, as I do not constrain and never abuse.
Now your life and journey and the quest of your soul,
Have tasks to complete, so fulfil then your goal.

> Away from the past to live in the present,
> Find your true heart and love, which shine evanescent.
> Karma and sin to cast aside like a stone,
> Return to the crown and be kept safe by my gown.
>
> For Angels and archangels, they watch every step,
> So, trust in your heart, and not in the head.
> Return to be 'still' and rejoice in the love,
> For the truth is within you ... not below or above.

Appreciate when you open your heart, mind, and soul's eyes together, your vision becomes clear, as one true being of light ... then, all is revealed, for no darkness or shadow can hide from the love that emanates and flows in every direction. Indeed, the illusion will be cast aside forever, so you can nurture and grow as the radiant spark you truly are, and as such, your magnificence, beauty, elegance, and divinity shall become glorified and untainted by anyone or anything.

This is what you are and always have been, but the eras and passing of time cloud the truth and this remained hidden from the world. However, the moment to erase and discard the past has arrived, and like an animal or insect shedding its skin, I urge you to reveal the new you ... cleaner, brighter, and more alive, and stronger than ever before.

You can achieve anything and everything, and nothing can withhold you from expressing true love, which waits to burst through from your heart's centre ... so re-ignite your inner spark and become the flame of hope and joy, which will carry you into eternity. Let all life bear witness to the truth both within and around you ... for when you do, others will then 'see' me in you too.

Truly, light flows from, through, and to you, so comprehend these bands of golden energy, which form rings around the earth and upon all places, are creating connections like links of a chain; entwined and embracing each other in friendship and peace and can never be broken. In fact, they are eternal, forged from and into my heart's fire, sealed with my grace and blessing to guide you towards eternal bliss ... along with a promise of this 'miracle' to have and behold, and cherish forever.

This cannot be erased or slashed by sword or tongue,
No matter if you are black, white, or whether old or young.
So, whether a pale yellow, or perhaps a shade of red,
Truth is beyond such trickery, of a so-called fear of death.

Please know your soul and goal, for you will then prevail,
From the impermanent world, find truth, so look right through the veil.
And if you are awake ... or deep within a sleep,
Seek the light, which shines bright, as day and night I both keep.
For inside is where you'll find every answer that you seek,
From me, who is the 'I', and the 'I am' who you now meet.

Amen.

LESSON 4:
RITUALS AND MONUMENTS

Ever since souls incarnated to the 'Earth-plane', you all embark upon the search for knowledge, wisdom and truth of me or 'I'. Even today, as millennia continue to drift by, an untold number of people (individuals, tribes, different societies) still seek this from the 'outside' world ... when in fact, everything one sees, hears, touches, smells or tastes (and intuition), always comes from within.

Remember, ever since humankind roamed through the ages, and long before the stone, iron and bronze eras began, they either looked around in awe and wonder upon the ground, or up into the sky ... amazed at the beauty captivating their minds and imaginations. Some knew their body is not the 'be all and end all', whilst others believed the future held only their deaths—without further consciousness and existence—and in fact, these are still the viewpoints from millions of people today.

Throughout time, those who appeared to be in 'control' created deities and God's ... holding power and influence over the many who would bend to their will, becoming too frightened to disobey or even question their thoughts and actions. As such, many of the wars upon Earth—along with the immense hate—become entrenched into one's mind-set and heart, leading to the decay, not only of society but also of the health and well-being of countless souls.

In addition, many hands built vast structures to both honour and please those who they believed created, saved, or fed 'life' itself. Sun Gods, rain Gods, and Gods of war and love were names to reverberate and resonate in temples, circles of stone, or monuments towering high above the horizon.

Different races of 'man' also made tracks or scorched the Earth to create lines and patterns over vast distances of land. These various shapes and images in all their glory only seen from the sky. They highlight the hopes and dreams of people who wanted to receive confirmation and approval for the deeds and actions of their nation.

Compare this to the present day, where the knowledge of human beings can expand through science and faith, and yet billions of people still understand so very little of love and light. The progress, quest, and journey of all can vastly increase, but only by sharing the truth you perceive and accept ... without hesitation, pride, jealousy, hatred, or any ego, too.

However, some may require constant approval, and will often seek illumination through complex rituals and behaviours, either in their daily activities or when they contemplate their life (or me). They even worship various statues, ornaments, and symbols, but this attachment is usually through an imaginary need and desire ... or it becomes a crutch to lean and support them during troublesome times.

Please comprehend, there are many cultures and civilizations throughout history depicting various religious figures, who guided (or indeed misguided) individuals or the masses. I am not suggesting that places of worship—built over many years—should be neglected or mistreated ... or that people should even banish or remove what can symbolize hope and peace for other hearts. No, only that I urge all those wishing to pursue their soul's path to bliss and peace to recognise their own divinity within ... and not through an impermanent figure, statue, building, or world.

Do not fret or imagine I am angry, because I am not. I only wish for you to realise the 'oneness' of all things, because a friend or neighbour, community or country is one and whole without division or separation. Each flower, rock, mountain, river, sea, and all things are I. When you clear fear and illusion away from the physical eyes—and the mind which plays tricks is subdued—you can sense everything is 'me'. Indeed, each petal, snowflake, tree, animal and insect, and every drop of an ocean's water are ingredients of my divinity.

Choices are always your own, but when the eyes of your body, mind, and soul are one, a clearer vision will reveal the pathway which lies before you. When this happens, you will no longer be walking in your own shadow, but it will be behind you forever. You will step into the light, walk in the light, and you will share in the light.

True beauty, therefore, lies deep inside you. It is beyond words, and no expression, picture, or image can convey what you are. You all contain the potential and the power to achieve the greatest gift of all, which is self-realization leading to liberation and bliss. Who or what can deny you but yourself? And no ritual or magic potion can ever relieve you of your karmic burden, or your soul's history through countless lives over hundreds, if not thousands, of Earth years? What you need to do is not easy, but neither are many worthwhile and everyday tasks in your life too.

Indeed, although numerous souls embark upon multiple incarnations, some will still state, "I can't get this right" ... but do not despair, and never anguish or fear one's actions if your heart and thoughts are pure, away from selfishness and greed, or self-gratification. Therefore, let light reflect from your heart's centre, and not what can seem a mirror of darkness and decay.

Please bask in the knowledge you can, and will, succeed. Believe in yourself and enjoy the path and road your life takes you ... for I will be by your side ... knowing, nurturing, guiding, loving, and forever watching over you. Let your smile beam joy towards all hearts, and let your hands do good, purposeful actions, which help and benefit others, too.

Do not seek greater rewards than you deserve, but sense the goodness (and not ego), shining back towards you. This is the true 'gold' you can wear with a higher value than any jewel or ring 'man' possesses, so appreciate you are richer in spirit and so much more ... a soul and light brighter than a thousand suns. Remember, humankind cannot perform any ritual or build any monument to match the gift of love you share with another. In addition, accept and recognize each other as one, because everything contains the spark and light of 'me'.

In this simple fact lies the answer to all things. By acknowledging, realizing, and living it, your lives will become more beautiful with each passing minute. I promise you, your dreams will come true, and you will only ever shed one tear ... a tear of pure joy, peace, comfort, and bliss, but do not try to describe the intensity of such, as this is a mistake. I love you all, as I now close this 'lesson' with a most heartfelt and pure, loving kiss. Amen.

LESSON 5:
POWER OF LOVE

You are I and I am you, and deep within, relearn this truth. Therefore, who is the King or who is the Queen ... only through searching and yearning, will you learn what I mean.

Now far away and yet nearer than near, live your own truth ... by not living with fear. For some of you doubt, upon this journey and road, but choices and decisions need the love of your souls.

In fact, your light is my light, and your life is mine too ... for all live in my heart, not only the few. Those illusions become shattered and now cast aside, as my peace washes over you, like an ever-flowing tide.

Indeed ... cleansing and purifying is the power of my love, while my grace lies in tears, which fall from within and above. These delicate drops of truth touch your lips, whilst your heart often aches ... just for one sweet embrace.

For no division can exist between both the 'you' and of I, unlike the differences and senses, like smell or of sight. As entwined are we and fixed upon the goal ... to stay within bliss, such a cherished soul.

Now angels of light, they sing out my name ... for in truth we are one, and 'all' are the same. So, hold on to those thoughts, yes purity of mind ... the truth for all life, all beings and 'mankind'.

For every creature of elements ... earth, water, ether, and fire, all resonates through me, and they will not tire. And they are no different, for only the 'body' has changed ... but as stated before; inside we're the same.

Indeed, human beings often think they are unique, when reality is the self ... in the 'I' where you seek. You may also seem different in skin colour or name, but do not be fooled, as this leads to shame.

So, inspire and aspire to behold now the truth, whether you're young or become old, and feel long in the tooth! Please try to be kind to those behind dark curtains or false screens ... as those veils of despair, only disguise what I mean.

Okay, let us move away from rhythm and reason ... and now appreciate that the Sun (and 'Son') rose yesterday, and they will rise again today and forever your tomorrow, across all planes, dimensions, and different places I created in love, light, and truth. With the knowledge nothing can truly 'die';

try to comprehend everything is, was, and always shall be.

Do not become deluded, and do not be cajoled into any other thoughts, feelings, or deeds to keep you from this reality. You are everything ... from the past, present, and into the future. Please realise, for every deception and all ills I am the cure, so believe in me; live in me ... because you are I.

Furthermore, understand you embark—and travel—upon the road that is only a flicker of so-called 'time', so your journey and life are mine too. Therefore, as I am light, love and all things, you cannot fade or cease to exist. The current 'clothes' in which your soul lives are vital, because the physical body enables you to remember, experience and know me, the 'Indweller' of your heart ... the one heart who can never part.

In all you do, try to be near and dear to me as I am to you, in the understanding you can offer me nothing, other than the flower and petals of your own heart's centre ... because all you ever were and are now, and what you can and will become, resides there. Do not be afraid either, for I cradle you in my loving arms and heart, but I am not like your birth parents holding their child, because this implies duality when none exists ... we are one, and always will be.

Appreciate the power of love is a universal beacon, one of joy, hope and of faith in me, and the same lives within you too. Its beauty is beyond compare, and though humankind's intellect cannot grasp this yet ... I am still your guiding hand of light, which will help you realise your higher self, the reality of 'you and me', the 'one'. All will comprehend this and understand what they require to 'become'.

With these words, the perception of your true being washes over you, and the bliss you sense lies eternal, as love is everywhere, in every place, and in all things. Indeed, you can always rest your soul upon my breast, for the same divine power beats as one within your chest, so open up the eyes of your heart to experience and share what you already possess. For now, be still and at peace ... in love and in light, good 'knight'. Amen.

LESSON 6:

STILLNESS

When you become 'still', you will feel love flowing from, through, and to all things ... and like the blood within your body and veins, I am the life force which enables you to carry out each activity of your soul, which helps you to accomplish everything your heart requires. My breath is the energy of creation too, and I am here for all life, all 'beings', and beyond 'time'.

If I am you and you are I, we cannot be divided ... nor separated, or broken. Therefore, we are whole. We are everything, nothing less and nothing more. Remember, you will appreciate this when you are at your most peaceful ... and by focusing upon the inner you, you focus on me, and then self-realization takes place.

In understanding this, you will fulfil your one true goal and dream ... into immortality of bliss and perfection, an embrace of pure love and light, captivating and enthralling you, as nothing else can or will compare. Everything else is pretence, false and impermanent, which so many people believe is the truth. No one can help another fulfil their own goal, as each one of you has a part to play ... and your own karma—body and action—to unfold.

Therefore, by becoming 'still', an opening arises for all Souls, like a doorway through the darkness, emerging into light ... and you undertake these journeys so the understanding, knowledge, experience, and enlightenment can follow. No boundaries exist when you continue with patience and forbearance, as only your own heart can place any limits upon oneself.

Please also realise, when you contemplate and reside in the purity of stillness, everything resonates in time together, as your vibration/energy, light and love connect with me. Subsequently, you receive and send power which spiral like a beautiful rainbow across time and space, love beaming brightly as it fragments into sparks of an eternal flame from a fire burning within ... which is a true marvel to comprehend and witness.

In addition, when you sit and wonder, perhaps contemplating upon everything around you, it is easy to forget the beauty 'within', put aside until another day, week, month, or year. Well, understand time resembles an everlasting river, carrying you along, but not to where you truly belong, which is with me eternally. Therefore, I wait, I wait, and I wait ... and because I am your shoreline and your rescue, you do not need to send an SOS for I am already here, inside your heart, and the recognition of such is all you need to help lead you to your timeless future.

Listen to my voice during the day, and at night while you are asleep. This is all you need to distinguish light within the darkness of the impermanent world ... it is the only 'light' you can comprehend and see in eternal truth. You will know implicitly and simply these things are true. Nothing else matters. Remember, when you become still, a thousand bells could chime, but you would only hear the truth from me. So then, what do you expect ... an awe-inspiring scene, a visual treat ... a miracle?

Well, I am the warmth if you are cold. I am the drink to quench your thirst. I am the light when you are blinded by darkness. I am the land encircling the ocean of doubt. I am the sky and clouds drifting by, watching over you. I am the mountain you climb in earnest, eventually reaching the peak, standing alone, yet entwined within my heart, you will be. I am the fragrance of sweetness from a flower. I am the air filling your lungs, and I am the touch caressing your face in a loving embrace ... indeed, I am everything and everything I am.

Understand this, you and I are one, and as such ... you are God, too. You become creation in action. This is a fact, not fiction, as I am the Indweller of your heart, and we never part. When all is said and done, your 'bodies' are but golden chariots, carrying you on your journey, so focus on the 'innerness' of you, but do not neglect both who and what your chariot is and does.

As human beings, try to be true to each other, and to the 'life' living with and around you, too. Do not succumb to lower senses, but rise above negative energies and situations, which can ensnare and encircle those who are unprepared. In fact, there is nothing you cannot achieve, as faith in yourself confirms your faith in me, so love yourself and your 'self' (the inner you) and accomplish your destiny.

In addition, try to avoid being deep-seated, rooted, and struggling, but spread your wing of love and light, taking flight into the well of your heart. This 'well' is eternal, the key to all things, and you will forever fly with me, because I am your other wing towards joy and peace.

Forget the fear of anyone or anything and embrace new opportunities which feel right (inside you) during your life. In tough times, I will support and carry and help you all I can. If in pain—for whatever reason—think of me. Yes, focus upon me and likewise, within your so-called happy times of laughter and joy, I will watch and sense the joy with you, too.

I am the answer to all your questions and queries, and all the missing pieces of your life's jigsaw, so when you see, feel, and know me, the 'picture' will be complete. No more 'returning' with a birth and death, and no further yearning or despairing, because you will desire or require nothing else ever again.

Therefore, be silent and listen to the bliss of peace. Wish and pray to find the truth, in the knowledge I am always with you and will never depart, for I cannot leave myself. By becoming 'still' you can remember, without exception, that I am love and light ... always and forever. Amen.

LESSON 7:
ENERGY

As your heart wells up with feelings of love, I bear witness to the grief which has beset you during the week. I am aware you sense me with more than your body too, because as your tears fall, they cling to my heart and divinity.

At these times—when you ache inside—I do not hide ... for I will lift you up with my grace and blessings to new heights, and ultimately bring smiles back to your face, so they may shine like beacons to all those who draw close from far and wide. Therefore, do not be sad, for Daisy is within me, protected by my love and kingdom, which encompasses all things, so do not suffer with pangs of guilt for which you both are clear.

Please understand your hopes and dreams will sometimes become nightmares, because fear leads to the perception and lack of control over one's destiny. This is strange, as you only need belief and faith in oneself ... the same you install upon me. Life is not always about fairy tales and happy endings, though it is easy to take one's joy for granted when they come true.

Know that one's life encompasses your body and your karma, and as such, your experiences occur before, with and by you, and they do so for your growth. In fact, these instances (or 'energies'), are all around you, working away as different vibrations and levels of ether, matter, and emotions of your 'being'.

Indeed, during those life stages of rebirth, education, employment, retirement, and old age, many types of energy will come into and around you. However, you cannot dissect, burn, erase, or hide what is part of creation. Why not consider and take this a step further by calling energy 'love', but how can you touch, feel, or even comprehend this? Well, in a simple analogy, can an innate object cry, laugh, or shout out aloud? No!

Understand I am all things in all places, and in every dimension. Because I encompass time, there is nothing I do not 'feel' ... therefore I sense anguish as readily as your joy. However, when people ask or pray to me, "Dear God, why have you not intervened?" one must comprehend (during grief and pain of the heart), such things are said with (or out of), anger, hatred, and desperation.

Through knowledge and experience—which leads to wisdom—you will find truth. In finding truth, you simply return to where you are from ... peace and true love. With practice, one must focus upon who and what they are, as well as what you think and say, because all deeds, thoughts and actions resonate through the ether, and they can either be positive or negative, resulting in helping, protecting, nurturing, and loving, or the complete opposite may occur.

Remember too, when you are 'still', try to contemplate and think of the body as a 'birth' and life force. In fact, your physical appearance is the only thing to be born, because of your divine essence, your Atma; your soul is permanent and cannot die ... only the impermanent elements of life fade and cease to live.

In contrast, by looking into the night sky, you may bear witness to a multitude of stars, all created from my love, but their energy changes over time. Some may even seem to disappear, to collapse and become black holes, yet they still exist, only in another form. A human body goes through similar processes; evolving, growing, maturing, but death always follows its birth. This 'vessel', (often cremated or buried), transmutes by fire and ash, or dissolved into earth. Timing is unimportant, as everything returns to me, for I am all things (which I will continue to reiterate).

Those who do not comprehend me in their hearts, I still love. Everyone is near and dear to me, and the realization of such, one day, will happen. All will sail upon my ocean of love, for I am the wind to empower those who flounder by the rocks. I will remove the anchor (and anger), weighing them down into the false position of a make-believe harbour within the physical world, with its materialism and traits of ego, personified by lack of compassion and mistrust.

This imaginary haven, which appears to protect you from the elements, can become a prison. Who says one can or cannot venture outside? Why such fear experiencing the new horizon, when this so-called sanctuary is an illusion of people's minds and hearts? It is a false energy, a harness holding one down, when in fact you are already free to live and experience eternal bliss.

Therefore, for one to progress, take a step towards me ... and to achieve what you think is impossible, take three. Subsequently, try to push aside those clouds of doubt by remembering to live inside my heart as 'one', and remove any confusion or feelings of separateness to each other.

I love you, and with every heartbeat (which echoes around the world), I am with you all ... so be 'still' to receive me. Never despair, for no one is alone, and I will always care. Please believe Daisy is safe in my hands, without suffering or fear, enveloped by peace and bliss, and try to live in the moment, by knowing and sensing me ... as I do you. Amen.

LESSON 8:
GRIEF, 'HEART-ACHE' AND THEN JOY

As you write the title of this passage, one may immediately think of a particular sequence of events must occur. From your own experiences, you appreciate this is not always the case, because true joy is within you, and is eternal too.

Therefore, no one needs to feel pain and anguish. However, before they can acknowledge this, the very nature of your mind (and the way you live), makes you believe this to be so. I state these things, because of the emotional rollercoaster you are both going through ... as Jasper, your beloved cat, suffering from old age and illness, passed away (your words, not mine). Please understand, his life on the physical plane would have faded some time ago, without your love washing over him through those years of togetherness.

When tears flowed, and your hearts ached in distress as he slipped away, angels and guardians (those who oversee all animals and creatures), escorted and carried him to peace and contentment within my light, which radiates for all beings. He is amongst his friends, and with those on the ethereal planes of vibration who know you both too. They are caring for him, so he is fine, and he will wait for you when you yourselves are ready to ascend and cross into your permanent state.

One must realise, 'Pud'—as you often called him—lived on the 'earth-plane' until his time to leave. Now, when you are grieving is most apparent, the mind tricks you, as all who imagine 'losing' their loved ones (be it relatives, friends, or pets), feel this trickery.

By now, you are experienced enough to deal with such things, as knowledge turns to wisdom. The love and light and acceptance of these events should now allow you to be unshaken, not by this, or indeed any other difficult circumstance. Some may believe this harsh of me, to suggest you need to overcome such burdens more easily, but this is what I am now asking you to do.

I will never ask you to abandon your feelings of oneness and love for another person, being, or a beloved pet, but what you should continually strive to achieve is the release of your attachment, and these are not the same thing. One may ask, "How can a devotee, an aspirant, or a disciple—looking for answers—define this with simplicity and clarity?" Well, the key is within yourselves, so all one has to do is to recognize and remember who and what you are, as stated many times before.

I understand it is easy to be deceived during stress and anxiety, but this is when your inner strength needs to prevail. Simply let go of negativity. Therefore, in terms of karma and right action, try to accept such events as occurring as they should, instead of the struggle to overcome a sense of separateness. Indeed, most people imagine they're divided, because they often state, "This is my husband, my wife, my child, and my pet", but in reality, they are not. They are all you and me, so we are 'one'.

In addition, many envisage a 'God' who presides over them, or one who lives in a particular place. They may even gaze upon a statue or alter which attempts to depict what I am … but if there is no separation, then I am all things, and all things are 'me'. Remember, I am a wilting flower and the next one to bloom. I am the tree without leaves, and the blossom that flies upon the wind. I am the desert and the seas, and I am the 'above and below'.

Through this reality, no one can ever be alone, not even in your darkest hour or even the happiest moment of your life. By comprehending this, should any 'death' occur, one must conclude the attachment is false, hence no loss or fear. This prevents anguish or grief, and without these, one can only shed tears of joy, celebrating a life who enriched your own, and all those who came to know them.

Remember, no one can erase or destroy the connection of love between two hearts, even if memory fades or time seems to erase what was once so strong. In fact, fire, water, earth, or sky cannot burn, erode, bury, or elevate this bond away, and because it is impossible to extinguish, there is no need to cry, no matter what the circumstances and events seem to conspire and bring to your 'door'.

Bear in mind the necessity to dilute the ego too, because false thoughts must not interfere with the process of truth … and your heart and soul cannot 'perish' by any man-made event either. I explain this because it is easy to conclude acts of violence—especially by so-called maniacs—as being void of divinity, but even a 'madman' (a perception made on earth), loves something or someone. People often find this difficult to come to terms with, or realise why, and how, a person could inflict pain or harm upon another.

Well, causes and triggers, such as pride, hate, anger, and jealousy burn deep within the psyche, and they lurk and hide within the shadows and recesses of the mind and body, looking for ways to express themselves, whereas love, compassion, kindness, and forgiveness need to grow inside the heart. These seeds of truth can multiply and expand, touching and reaching far beyond the boundaries of any imaginary walls, whether they are physical, mental, or emotional, so live with dignity and those values enabling you to be called a human being.

You are all so special; therefore, strive to be the best person you can be. Any job or activities you engage in are all by-products, and these, if undertaken honestly and truthfully, are for the well-being of your fellow man and society. Remember, every act of kindness reverberates like chimes of a bell, for they echo and expand upon waves of love and light.

With this knowledge, your hearts do not need to bear hurt and fear or cry out for tears to fall in pain. Try then, not to miss or despair when 'letting go' of someone (or a pet) but continue to rejoice and sing their name in praise, for the wonderful opportunity and time you had together in the plane of existence you currently reside upon. Therefore, please appreciate this Easter, I shall be:

- The boat, which carries you across the ocean(s) of your emotions.
- The land you walk upon holding you upright and true.
- The wind, to blow dark clouds away from your body, mind, and soul.
- The spiritual 'vision' to reveal the light ... and the Sun to radiate warmth and love in your heart.
- The hand that lifts you up from the ground when you feel you cannot go on.
- The life giving 'water', to quench your thirst for truth, knowledge, and wisdom.
- The spark deep within you, which gives you everlasting life.
- The colours of the rainbow, shining down upon your darkened days of false fears and tears.

We are '**one**' forever, so please do not grieve. Erase the heartache and pain, as you are eternal joy ... now live, breathe, know, and understand this. Appreciate love conquers all things that you could ever possibly imagine fearing ... so do not, as you are nearer than near to me. I love you all. Amen.

LESSON 9:

JOY OUT OF DARKNESS

The depths of the night, the deep, the abyss, or you could even say hatred, are all names one may use to describe 'negativity' and fear. In contrast, understand there will always be the 'positivity' and light ... bringing balance to all walks of life, both within and upon every planet, dimension of time and space, and in all vibrations (energy) too.

Therefore, even in your darkest hour, nothing can deny or erase the glimmer of hope that exists, because nothing can destroy true light and love.

Throughout 'time', people have written or spoken about these facts, but these are often in confusing, over-elaborated text, or even symbolic in nature. However, one must realize the **key** to truth, knowledge, and wisdom is simplicity ... and your 'heart' is the **lock.** Once combined, these reveal a true insight into my love.

Appreciate too; when those soft, musical notes flow around the room in which you sit, they energise and vibrate with immense purity. These are not material or transient to the physical but move in waves of peace towards all who gather, read, or hear these words, and within these moments, no bewildered looks of expression settle here. Even if a soul seems lost, confused, or at the point of giving up ... their spark can still illuminate, so at this Easter time, a special reflection of your faith will mirror in many a heart's flame.

Remember, when Lord Jesus was crucified, the heavens went black. Many believed the world was ending, screaming out, "How could the Saviour die? Why did he not save himself? Why did God not save his Son?" Of course, on the third day, Jesus ascended from the impermanent plane upon the Earth, and hence 'joy came out of the darkness'.

He had indeed endured the most incredible pain, not only from the cross, but also inside his heart by the very people he had come to guide ... and lead back to me. Please comprehend his experience was necessary and ordained by me, acted out by destiny and fate to guide you from the depths of shadow and into the light.

In fact, to clear unbalanced karma (and find him), simply enter your true heart, for the Lord sits in the seat of every soul. He is part of the eternal flame of golden love, and his magnificent light emanates and permeates in all directions, flowing in a constant, gentle stream, washing and wearing away the rocks of your sin you yourselves created. This will gradually erode or instantly make it vanish, for purity and truth shine without boundaries, and can conquer all fears and ills.

Please note, sometimes the imbalance resembles granite because of the depths of darkness residing there. In addition, many lifetimes may need to be undertaken for this to be dissolved by the bearer, because many lessons must be learned through themselves, or by—and for—those they live, meet or work with, or even those strangers who pass by in the blink of an eye.

Over time, though, even this turns into dust, similar to your physical bodies, until 'you' become 'balanced' in every sense of the word. Remember though, even dust leaves a trace, and so does the memory of each lifetime and journey, which is your legacy.

This Easter, try to rediscover your inheritance, for the reconnection to bliss may even form part of one's deepest, darkest hour. You only require an open heart, free will, compassion, and forgiveness, but are these all too much? No! For such things are within you all, so please act upon them once they have been recognised 'inside' oneself.

Therein lies the choices you can make, and these are clear for the soul. The Lord did not falter in his quest, goal, and 'work' to bring my love, vision, insight, and light to you all. In recognising the truth upon the cross, you rediscover your own: one light and one love within all … from all … and to all.

Once known, the individual must discount and deny, or embrace and accept, who, what, and the why they 'exist'. Remember, when sunshine falls upon your face, you feel uplifted, happy, content … but when the eternal light radiates and rests inside your heart, you will realise you are already complete.

Imagine the happiness and smiles from distraught parents when they find their lost child, or the stranded airlifted to safety …. perhaps the discovery a loved one—though trapped—is both alive and well. One may comprehend these scenarios and many more like them, but even these are fragments of elation compared to the feeling of oneness, and the glory of love and light.

So, after fulfilling your life's work and karma and destiny, you will eventually cross over into the permanence of me, which is your 'homecoming'. However, this is not a game or a roll of the dice but entered voluntarily and willingly by all souls.

Indeed, you have all required 'time' to complete what you need to do, so use this wisely in whatever you wished for (and required) to become the best human being you can be. Release your never-ending supply of my love … for truth, honesty, compassion, and forgiveness. Be what you all were, are and always will be, a part of my expression, shining both peace and joy out of the darkness!

A SOUL'S GOAL

You strive to be 'one', yet you are already free,
And your soul is a branch or a leaf on the tree.
To then float upon the breeze and be taken by free-will,
Though sometimes you will struggle to climb up life's hill.

You journey alone, and yet we are never apart,
While a connection is in truth if the heart is ajar.
And like a door so strong, made of fine spiritual oak,
Enter and be bathed, by my joy; lie and soak.

Emerge and sustain in your new zest for life,
Be gentle and kind; love your friend, husband, or your wife.
So, walk the good walk and talk the good talk,
And be true to your soul to fulfil your true 'goal'.

Amen.

LESSON 10:
THE 'GOAL'

To date, we've looked at small segments of information, which briefly described the purpose of your earthbound existence and current embodiment, because of your karmic 'imbalance'. I explained these to help quench your continuing thirst for knowledge and wisdom at this time of your lives, because people often go from day to day and year to year without venturing past minor doubts or misapprehensions.

One should realise, taking a small step to self-realization is better than none, and those who deny I exist are only distancing themselves too far from me (within their minds or thoughts), because deep inside their hearts, they would recognise me instantly.

I am not chastising anyone, no matter what someone chooses to be or does. The important issue (in any situation or event) is whether what's said or done is with truth and honesty, which reveals your true character, and is the net result of your thoughts, words, and deeds.

Therefore, by denying love and light exists, they resemble a 'zombie', living in shadow … hiding and pretending to see in the dark. In these examples, the only truth to be seen or felt is from within oneself, and a 'spiritual' magnifying glass or microscope would be needed to focus upon their core flame, which has become dimmed, but still effulgent with beauty and elegance beyond compare.

You all have choices to make, and to do what is good and true. Many will still ask, "How can we constantly remember how to act and live in truth, always doing the right thing within such a fast-paced and sometimes disturbing world?" Well, the answer is always simple, so I will explain this in rhyme and reason to you.

> Right or wrong are words in a song,
> For truth is the way, from youth to old age.
> So, do what you feel and feel what you do,
> As tears that fall are from 'one', not two.

Please discuss, meditate, or let each sentence wash over you, because life can be as simple or as complicated as you make it ... so try to be content in whatever circumstances you find yourselves. This does not mean you cannot strive and accomplish your hopes and dreams but aim to become satisfied with who and what you are in all areas of your mind, body, and soul. (Remember, these may appear separate, yet are whole, as they affect and influence each other).

Appreciate the mind can be a true friend or can lead you up the 'garden path' towards illusion and the confusion discussed many times before. Your thoughts can often betray you, to disguise the reality that is only a breath or heartbeat away. Therefore, I ask, do you let your senses control you, or do you control them?

In realising this, you can put the right processes into place, to quell any false desire of what you think you want and need. For instance, by becoming more positive in your outlook and approach to life, you will initiate greater sources of information and guidance, as these often reach those who first search for themselves. No one is 'out on a limb', because help and love are there for everyone, and when the body, soul and mind work in unison, all will truly see this.

Understand too, your body is impermanent and dying the moment the physical is 'reborn' ... therefore, it is important to look after it, in order to help you achieve so much more in your life. In addition, others may call a person's body 'incomplete' ... but do not believe you are any less a person (or being of light and love), within the eyes of my heart.

Realise everyone is whole to me, and your history and karma playing out has no bearing on whether you deserve to succeed in your true goal or not. Though this is a fact, people can do stupid things for crazy reasons, so each of you are responsible for the choices you make at any point in your life.

Regarding the impact of such things upon a soul—and I stated this long ago—those who were evil would remain accountable, and to create ... or rather restore balance (though some may say 'punishment'), could even lose their soul memories. In this respect, do not think of me as a controlling entity, someone who is head of a class to punish or praise ... but, if I were to say I cannot do such things, would you think me weak, powerless to intervene in any way shape or form?

For now, try to think about this in simpler terms, such as a parent who berates their child for misdemeanours they carry out. Please understand, one's spiritual education is not about the 'carrot or the stick', but of your own inner responsibilities, character, and expression of divinity ... so you in fact live through, and by, your own scales of justice.

With these thoughts, you should know I am 'pure' love and light. So, your own freewill was not granted/ given permission by any governing body or higher power... other than by whom and what you—and me—already are.

For this reason, all your reaction to action, and your cause to the effect, can be nothing more than this. Therefore, each soul can shine brightly as a billion suns, or as a dim light, covered by a blanket of hate and doubt.

Please realise, in order to remove such impediments, simply tug or pull them away as quickly as you can, as if you were removing a thorn from your foot or finger ... because the relief from anguish and pain is instantaneous, like a morphine injection. Your life will become free of those false desires, which bound and held you through the pretence of embodiment, while self-realization and the goal ahead reveal the shining glory to wear like a crown ... majestic and brilliant, reflecting both within and without all the love you behold.

You must seek the 'goal' from inside you, as this is the only way to succeed. You will not find your answers in any other human being, as every embodiment, no matter how loving, how peaceful, or how beautiful, has their own karma to balance and their own life and road to follow.

All books and literature of any religious persuasion can only act as guides, helping you to realise the need to discover the reality yourself. No one, or any 'thing', should insist you cause pain to any other element of life. Remember, so you sow so shall you reap, and even though this may appear not to happen upon this earth-plane, karma will always play its part to uphold truth and balance in every dimension and vibration level that exists.

Therefore, to reach fulfilment, bliss, and peace in me is destiny, which circumnavigates across every sinew of your being. This is inherent inside you all, even if no sign of this choice or search is shining upon the exterior 'body'. In fact, the spiritual link and our connection are finer, and far more complex, than any scientist's equation or DNA sequence ... yet with all things considered, is still simpler and much easier than a child's 'ABC'.

I urge you to ignore all fear (as this feeling can only trap and bind you), and to comprehend you are 'love' ... to love, by love, in love, and through love. If you deny this, then you are also denying me ... but if you accept your true self, you are accepting me with all your heart, soul, and mind, and in all things, too. Indeed, this is the simplest explanation of them all. Amen.

LESSON 11:

THREE

Within the silence, thoughts and feelings now emerge, but are these from the mind, the heart or from both? Perhaps our love transmutes, and then releases these from your soul? Well, today I will explain and let you digest what I mean regarding these things, as many people who read and contemplate upon this will discover a greater understanding of what is involved, and the process by which they need to strive and pursue to reach their true goal.

Therefore, someone thinking of the word 'three' may initially think of the numerical number or perhaps engage in a deeper expanding thought. This could range from simple numerology or by considering the power encompassing mind, body, and spirit; the Father, Son and Holy Ghost ... and even faith, hope and charity. Someone may express or describe each of these elements as the Holy Trinity, but please put any preconceptions to one side. In order to simplify life, one must try to understand ... man, beast, and God.

During the rituals of working, eating, and sleeping, as well as those thoughts, words, and deeds you subconsciously and consciously engage in ... all contain both choices and decisions to make, and each takes one of the aforementioned forms. In fact, not only one but also all three can control your desires, hopes, and dreams.

If you kindly help another living thing, do you realise what has actually taken place? When hurtful actions, words, or thoughts have manifested themselves far beyond your four walls, are they human, godly, or of a beastly trait? Regarding your daily situations, try to place what they imprint on the mind and contemplate the direct result and outcome of such things ... or simply let the 'impression' of the information drip through to your consciousness and fall upon your heart.

In addition, consider whether the feelings and thoughts of 'desire'—whether they are material, mental or physical—are degrading the resulting actions you take? Does the need or dependency (in its various forms) envelope and make you feel different in any way? When you analyse these, do they reveal any lowering in the vibration and energy of your soul?

Some say they do, as one can become animalistic, 'beastly' and even 'ungodly'. Therefore, if you choose the resulting consequence of all your actions, thoughts, and deeds, then one must strive for only one eventuality, and this should be 'godly'. Is this easier said than done ... of course it is!

The inquirer, the aspirant, or the devotee must always consider the outcome, and in doing so, which of the 'three' will prevail. In reality, for every soul to reach the goal of eternal bliss in me, then a divine result must be the number one priority ... the winner, and the master of all things. Do not waver or doubt your success. If you were to think of such as a race, some will give up. Others get side-tracked, taking what they believe are smoother roads when none exist.

How long does this take? Well, did the tortoise not beat the hare in the tale and fable? For instance, you may find the path you take is short, but for some, it means their whole lifetime. Remember, do not class your own road and journey above another's, because each of you live with your own karma to balance and work through. So do not judge; lest ye be judged.

Try to eliminate any concerns over 'time', in terms of your days, weeks, months or years, as it waits for no man, and you cannot alter this. Comprehend I am the shoreline and your harbour instead, for within me—and you—are where you will find eternal rest and peace.

Understand too, as each morning breaks, and the Sun rises in the phenomenal world, the light brings warmth and substance to all living things. In the same way, the illumination of your heart and soul radiates and reflects all you are, have been, and will be. Your whole being can reveal these as human, beast, or godly actions and qualities.

This is important, because as you grow and mature, these 'three' elements become expressed through your character, personality, and attitudes, and in fact, with everyone you meet too. Indeed, every environment or situation will cause you to think and react in the way described.

Only by experiencing the truth of your search (during daily life), dictates the outcome. Remember, your divinity holds no doubts, and shares no blame or shame, and while the outer casing (which is your body) conceals the beauty and peace, it still allows the illusion and confusion to rain through, too. Therein lies the choice ...from deep inside you.

Please appreciate, at Christmas, people seem to despise, want, or need something, which is usually in the material sense. For example, picture a child ripping open a present, fervently casting aside the wrapping paper in their eagerness to see the 'prize' inside. Through their enthusiasm to reveal and know what it contains, they take no time to see who sent it, and some parents (or next of kin) may become annoyed or even anguished by this, citing their child's sheer excitement got the better of them. Everyone should have this same desperation and yearning, but for the gift of love, light, and truth instead ... and I too wish you all to experience the joy, unveiling what you so desperately seek and need.

In reality, the outer 'wrapping' (over the true you), is impermanent, and is therefore cast aside to be buried or burnt. Well, I am not concerned with everything that envelopes your divinity within, for your looks, appearance, and material wealth are all by-products and unsustainable. On one's rebirth and embodiment, you possess nothing of the material world you enter, and so you return 'without' too. Only the essence and growth of your soul and being remain intact, and your karma will have played its part in balancing, erasing, or even multiplying this.

In the earlier example, the child did not wait to see who gave them their gift, whereas true love—which is you—cannot be labelled. No tag is required in order to express a 'to' and 'from' ... because love is, was, and always will be.

Indeed, love is in all creation and both you and me. It is this, above all things, that makes you 'godly', and because of this; is the element of the 'three' that will live forevermore. Therefore, in peace and blessings live your today, for you are my gift and the present—I have pre-sent—for we are all one. Amen.

LESSON 12:
A CHRISTMAS CAROL

As you sit and become still, you can sometimes sense the pressure in and around your head, and often people say this occurs when receiving communication from the so-called 'dead'. Please understand, though, when one is quiet and still, other souls may draw close to you from all walks of life ... and with different energies, too. This is because they wish to partake and learn, for not only do they listen, but they sense the information and love you give and send from both inside and out, too.

In fact, when experiencing any natural or unnatural phenomena, this exposes you to many feelings, leading one to make different conclusions. Therefore, while people often think they are alone, this cannot be so, and I shall keep reiterating this until it becomes etched deep within your psyche.

When something is right for the individual (or for those bearing witness nearby), then a resonance, a spark, and a true feeling of joy and fulfilment transpires inside the heart. Through these experiences, you will understand I am helping you upon your journey and quest to rediscover and desire your permanence with me in all aspects of your being.

Now, with these forthcoming festivities, I hope the masses will celebrate with open hearts, able to share and sow new seeds of love, which can grow and harvest when required to do so. Those of you with Christian beliefs will often bring a Christmas tree into the home, and whether real or artificial, adorned it with decorations and the like. However, this reflects the truth, for only nature can produce those needles (which can be soft and gentle or hard and sharp) and bear so much more.

A tree such as this grows into a wonderful shape, and while living, displays an aura of luminosity, which is something to behold. In essence, the light manifests from all points and radiates in every direction. It is both beautiful and serene, resembling a star ... created by and from love.

I explain this to you because of the stresses and strains one brings upon oneself (because of commercial, materialistic, and family pressures), and only when you relax and be at 'one', with the same light and ambience as the pine tree, can this manifest itself to touch those around you. Remember ... happiness, joy, peace, goodwill, friendship, forgiveness, and compassion for another soul or being are all magnified and personified when truth flourishes from within.

So, during this special atmosphere of love and light, be like the pine tree's branches, and extend your arms and heart to another. May you reach the broken-hearted, to become a beacon for those who find the courage to cast aside their doubt and look for guidance. With nurture and nature going hand in hand, and with so many aspects of a human being's life just like this ... in time, all will understand who and what they really are.

Now then, as Christmas day approaches, many people will gather in the name of the Lord and sing praises of—and for— 'God's love'. They come together for many reasons, but their hearts and souls all become soothed by the uplifting hymns and carols. Such words can bring a simple meaning to a person, but for another, it could be the 'sensing of', or even a heightened awareness of much more than this.

Indeed, over the millennia and eras of time, souls gathered in worship and prayer too many a so-called 'God', with some civilizations believing there was a supreme being or deity in one form or another, something far greater than they could imagine. However, when you accept and understand I am creation, wisdom will stem from what is already inside you.

Therefore, even if you bear witness to amazing scenes, images, or celestial events (such as a solar eclipse), which are all physical and impermanent, this does not matter, because when you sense and accept them through your heart, the Soul receives the key. This allows you to remember and experience in whatever way makes sense of 'me' ... for I am love, and love is everything.

For today, this lesson will be shorter in terms of 'knowledge' to be shared, and I therefore pause in liaising with you. Try to reflect upon Christmas with a poem, prayer, or a carol, and decide what part such words play in your heart.

A Christmas Carol

Two hearts that beat as one,
Louder and louder, they do become.
Linked in truth and by hand in hand,
Travelling through time to a promised land.

Your souls drift by in search of the Son,
To pass through love of the enlightened 'one'.
And with knowledge and wisdom given freely to all,
Open hearts and arms wide when you hear the call.

As time waits for no man, beast, or being,
I am the truth, all perceiving and all seeing.
All you have to do, is to realise we are one,
Your immortality and bliss, in truth, you have won.

For your goal has been set, and it's the path you now take,
One's past lives and history are not now at stake.
It is the present you are given, unlike under the tree,
To find victory, not defeat, and be forever in me.

Our love and our light, which encompasses all things,
Is not manufactured by hands or made by machines.
For the ingredients of your body, and of the 'physical' world,
Are always erased, like I said and have told.

Please then go forth, with a spring in your step,
Try to renew your own faith, no matter what you 'get'.
And as long as you hold on, with true love in your heart,
Eternal life my true gift, and never to part.

Peace, love, and blessings to you all,
Amen.

LESSON 13:

PEACE AND GOODWILL

Love and light and truth and kindness flow to each one of you, but what you are and can yet become still depends upon your thoughts, words and deeds. Would you say this is your own freewill, or by the Divinity within you, which enables you to shine more brightly, offering peace and balance to those whom you meet?

I state this so you do not think relationships, acquaintances, or meetings of like minds happen by chance, when in fact you are often guided to go where you are needed most ... both your own and for another's experiences. Consider this not as fate, but the pathway to greater things.

Please understand too, although words such as destiny, nirvana, and bliss try to describe one's journey and goal, everything you say carries the power to either uplift another's heart ... or when spoken in anger—or with hate—cut down the very soul, which reflects your own and me. Therefore, by seeing the divinity in everything, you are bearing witness to your true 'self' too.

In reality, when also assisting and helping others, spirals of energy—formed through love and light—swirl from inside and above you, like a DNA helix both touching and melting within the vibration and resonance of creation. These can travel through all dimensions, time, and space, far beyond your phenomenal world and earth-plane too. It is a fact, not fiction, when coming from a true heart. Nothing can erase or break it in two, for it is all pervading.

Right now, many of you are preparing for Christmas, which is a season for peace and goodwill. However, as I mentioned once before, this can be a worrying period for many reasons, not least to those whose hearts radiate with despair, frustration, or fear. In most situations though, a helping hand is all it takes to lighten the load, or by offering forgiveness and compassion, give strength and hope to another ... but in whatever form, know this gesture is a spark, re-igniting the peace to flourish inside a heart.

Remember, if you assist in truth, not only does the recipient benefit, so do those who gather and witness the event too. This is because kindness indirectly magnifies within the aura and timeless energy surrounding it. Do not become confused or misinterpret these things, though, because our connection is eternal, sustained by the 'to and fro' of a beating heart of light.

Please try to become more aware of such opportunities, as 'looking' with physical eyes alone; they often pass unnoticed. Overall, by living a life of unconditional love, everything opens up before you. In fact, what then evolves in and around you are so magnificent that some regard as miracles in themselves.

What do you need to do in order to activate these wonderful things? Well, why speak when a smile or hug can show how much you care. Ask yourself right now, when someone crawls upon hands and knees in total despair, and their heart and soul seem torn in two, what can you do?

I urge your love to draw closer, and let it be a candle of light within their darkest hour. Shine forth like a beacon and draw back the veil of illusion and bewildering pain of confusion, which entraps and grounds them. May your kindness be there when it's needed most, and if you believe it to be true, it will be, I promise you. (The recognition of this gracious act may not be perceived straight away but is felt far beyond the senses of the people close by).

In terms of one's development, their personal journey and quest, you will always find me 'inside' your heart ... where peace and goodwill reign supreme; and nothing can detract from this. By searching within, one can be happiest and most content you can ever be, and this does not exist upon the phenomenal world, as nothing is permanent there. In stillness, you discover we are forever ... eternal and everlasting, and with a true understanding of being 'one' without separation or division. Such joy can, and will, radiate for all, and only the 'timing' taking place on the earth-plane detracts from this.

Therefore, what do the masses wish and yearn for at this festive time? Many hearts will cry out, "I want peace"—in the belief it is previously unattainable—but take away the ego (I), the desire (want) ... and they will leave you with peace. So too, by removing the immorality you have immortality, and goodwill transcends to 'God's' will.

One must comprehend there is no need to suffer or fear at all, just have faith in yourself and not in false desires or greed. Share your limitless love, and you will see the effects upon the lives of those around you, and indeed, also on your own.

Please try to see the beauty and the magnificence of the truth, as the light within shall reveal the golden path which leads you to me. I am always waiting and never hiding, and my open heart and arms will cradle you in bliss ... all you have to do is believe, as I have said so many times before.

Know me, like I know you,
Want me, like I want you,
Trust me, like I trust you,
Understand me, like I understand you,
Believe in me, like I believe in you.

Then truly discover me, your secret treasure,
Keeping me close, for we are 'one'.
Remember me always, in all things said and done,
No separation, no division, and just become.
Amen.

LESSON 14:
STAR OF WONDER

Welcome once more to one and all, but deep inside the heart, can you really hear my call? For I am here, there, and am everywhere … even beside you in the next chair ... and always within and never without, so why do you wish to scream and shout?

Do not believe in false riddles or jokes, during the time for high spirits, so be careful not to choke. And as Christmas arrives at your home and your heart, why do many souls now cry and fall apart?

With so much stress and cause for '*dis*-ease', as one-half stands and others bend knees. Though forgiveness and joy do the many now wish, others look blank as they cross off their list. They ask shall I give, or will I receive, when the truth reveals ... 'you all get what you need'.

The hungry and the poor simply cry out in vain, as those who walk by, sometimes glance of disdain. So, who is the happier as both expressions had met … the rich in the wallet or within heart instead?

Do you shine as the 'hustle' and the 'bustle' pick up pace, with cards to write, and oh so many calls to now make? Can you radiate and glisten as the 25th draws near, or does the eve and the day, bring out dread and new fears?

For you all have a decision, to glow like the 'Son', each day and by night, until your victory is won. So please try wearing smiles, with new selfless frowns, or do you take party frocks and trade them all in for nightgowns?

However, to hide light away so that no one can see, just disguises the real you, and of course the real me. For a wardrobe so deep, displays the true choice, as garments masquerade, like a change in your voice. Indeed, you can even dress up, in whatever one likes, but the truth of it all, the world grips like a vice.

Therefore, who holds you in place; for it must only be self, contained in four walls, not by goblins or elves. So, I urge you to walk, and find new chinks of light, the way out and way in, as its love at first sight.

For you can discover, a new freedom and expression, as open hands lay before … you will realise the score. The eternal goal you must reach, in unison and as one, for all can move on to live and become.

With the pathway I set, countless eons ago, laid out before you, as your heart will now know. With many people and new friends, to come into your life, some will stay single, or take husbands or wives.

All are entwined as fragments of me, and everyone is linked and must return to the tree. Like branches and twigs, you reach out near and far, as relatives and kin, travel through time, not by car.

Throughout creation and the universe, love reigns supreme ... opened hearts and minds know of just what I mean. Please trust within me, to search and discover, what lies in the distance, but not undercover.

With galaxies and constellations, too many to mention, simply expand your horizon ... isn't that your intention? For the stars and the planets, they all mesmerise, but the truth is inside, and not seen with your eyes.

It is beautiful and magnificent, no earthly words could describe ... glittering prize to behold, and only beyond mind. For thoughts often trick you, into thinking what is best, forget false desire, as love does the rest.

So, while looking at the sky, upon dark starry nights, what do you wish for or fear, go to ground or take flight? Is your head in the clouds, as some state you are, or is your heart far above, so-called madness of crowd?

One should be who you are, and what you were born unto be ... an expression of love, made of you and of me. Do not pass into shade, of past duties or time, rather walk to the glory, of the light so divine.

For every moment or step, which you take towards me; the closer I become, for I shall take three. Sincerely I wish, for your good conduct in life ... no ultimatum or test but living in love is the best.

My grace is abundant, and is forever please trust, so having faith within me, and inside, is a must. So, rise above times, when you cry or breakdown, for I will protect you forever, with light from my crown.

When my 'glory' shines down, some hearts may not feel, if you then turn away, from friends and family who are real. By linking arms and your hands, with neighbours as one, the world can still change, and it has already begun.

This is hard to be seen, and for you to realise when violence and hatred seem forever to rise. Therefore, do not succumb, to what the media or politics portray, but do all that you can, to help lead man from decay.

With everyday choices and these are your own; try leading by example, and not by false throne. Act then in truth, to achieve the extra mile, for always I am with you ... whether meek or the mild.

No matter if an adult, even teenager or child, what is your dream, and what makes you smile? And if I made ... your one wish come true, what would you ask me, and is it for you?

More money, a job, new clothes, or new life, perhaps a change of your body, but not by a knife? Do not become down, by any trouble and strife, or think you are unloved, because that is not right.

Because you are everything and in truth come from me, not separate, or divided, for that could not be. Indeed, your essence and your beauty cannot be called into question, no matter what debate or arguments are mentioned.

For you and I both know, this all to be true, simply put we are 'one,' so do not feel shame or be blue. This Christmas time, then, please forgive and forget … the pain or the anguish, by which karma may have set.

Instead, please be joyful and reach out from your heart, as true love is eternal, and there from the start. As in the past and the present, it's time to decorate your home, live to the full and in peace … beyond speech or the phone. For the star of wonder, you now place upon the tree, represents a 'life' beyond dreams, and is your true reality!

Happy Christmas to you all.
Amen.

LESSON 15:
MISSING YOU

After the previous 'uplifting' lessons, some may believe they have come back down to Earth ... a reality check of normal daily living, but why would I do this though?

Well, time and time again during the festivities (and with a New Year approaching), I bear witness to unified hearts, feelings openly displayed, crying in joy. Numerous people, though, still wish to forget the past, trusting and hoping in what a change of date will bring them, because they grieve with tears of disbelief, fear, and trepidation. Indeed, this can be a difficult period, in particular for those who miss loved ones, and I understand this.

It is plainly obvious; two hearts will appear to be separated only when this knowledge is rejected—or not yet grasped—and here I sense and feel so much pain from the broken. Tears flow and pour from their aching wounds deep within, and this pierce me like sharpened knives. In essence, while minds are numb and emotions raw, one's eyes remain closed as deafening screams of anger or disbelief take hold. Remember, as we are 'one', your pain is my pain, and your joy is my joy too.

Whether someone's anguish and so-called loss or separation occurs through the death of a loved one ... true love is eternal. What I speak of is inside your hearts. It is beyond all things. The passage of time cannot erase or break it. Distance becomes a false boundary. No one can manufacture this in some worldly place, and neither can you buy, sell, deceive, persuade, or cajole unconditional love, because purity is not 'born' and therefore cannot die. It is, was, and always will be.

Realise and appreciate that those who mourn at this time of year may often wish for hope, as they ask or pray for my help, or even forgiveness for something they should or should not have done. However, I will not go into further detail about such requests.

Across the world, many people seem lost, or hide themselves away. They are often confused or become 'used' by someone who they may or may not even know. Perhaps ego or guilt plays a part, particularly in those who look and gaze into the night sky for celestial inspiration and guidance.

Similar to a lightning bolt, which moves across an immense distance to strike the ground below, one's thoughts can also travel and explode into sparks of anger, hate, jealousy, and pride, causing havoc and destruction to those who are directly in the line of fire. In addition, they can reach way beyond the intended individual or recipient. All of this has consequences, because there is no action without reaction, or cause without effect.

The person who receives may well be shocked, but what is being returned to the source? Well, all will depend on whether the soul and person can rise above any pain from the resulting reaction, words, or heartache. In each scenario, one should always think of me. You do not have to request my divine help to intervene; you only need to think of the love within you, and in every other being.

However, souls often ask forgiveness for another, or even for oneself, so do not become confused by what I now explain. If I were to say to you, I do not forgive, this will sound bizarre and strange, but it is true. I love you, and mercy and compassion are already there for you, inside your heart, and not found by some magical act or miracle.

Each heart can bleed in more ways than one, so feelings of guilt and blame by another's actions may seem too much to bear. The confusion and delusion set in, and so it becomes easy to miss the point in what you are saying, thinking, feeling, and truly sensing.

In reality, this is the 'all', yet it is far easier to believe you are different to each other, with diverse goals, desires, and wants. This illusion only evaporates when focused upon the truth, as the heart contains the same core essence of light, love, and me. As a result, when hearts connect, they remember they are part of everything, both beautiful and all-encompassing. If one could bottle this up, you would label it the divine essence, or an elixir of life itself.

Consider once again those who appear to be separated, to be reunited in a wonderful embrace ... a young child missing from their family, or even a son or daughter who returns from a far and distant place to find their parents waiting for them. Alternatively, perhaps a husband and wife, or a partner and their lover, having searched so long for each other, finally meet and kiss once more. In another example, someone who is missing a beloved pet, and they are returned or find their own way home. These are but a few of the many instances and circumstances I could mention.

Realise at this precise moment of connection (or reconnection), their joy is beyond comprehension, an out-pouring of emotion and love, which radiates like a starburst or a supernova, and can be sensed through time and dimension ... beautiful.

For those who have not experienced this yet, do not become disturbed or dismayed, as this can be hard to comprehend when the bond of true friendship seems broken or divided. However, one needs to believe and trust and know me in yourself to appreciate all is well, for I do not wish for any soul to feel sadness, anguish, and pain either. (I will not explain or go into further detail regarding karma, but this reality must remain firmly etched within your mind).

One day, upon reaching your goal and divine resting place—permanently within me—those who missed love will also find bliss. This is my promise to you all, so do not fear and worry. Those who have faith and comprehend what I say already believe I hold their hand, and equally, those who currently cannot grasp such guidance need to know I will not neglect them either. No one is lost ... so all you need to do is to remember whom and what you are to live and 'be' the truth. By opening up from within, you will see through the mist and doubt of despair ... to realise I care and love you forever.

I entitled this lesson as 'Missing You', because after all I have said ... I do. This may seem bizarre, when I always reiterate, we are 'one', but the fact is, I need you to grow and know who and what you are and can be. Every one of you is unique and amazing, and so much more can be achieved as an individual soul and through all humankind too.

Your life's journey can appear good, bad, or indifferent, one of hardship or even basking in success, but try to understand everything is for love, only love. Therefore, do not despair or grieve, but remember the joy from, through and to the well of your heart.

Those tears falling from your face, I will bless with my grace. Any feelings of an aching, breaking heart, I will wash away with my own. Become 'still' then, and instantly notice our togetherness, the oneness of me and of 'us', no separation, only unity. There you will be purified and glorified into eternity. You will not miss me, for I will not be missing you. In love and light, be at peace. Amen.

LESSON 16:
ACCEPTANCE

I welcome one and all and will start today's lesson with some questions. Whenever the New Year is upon you (within the physical and impermanent world), how will a change in numbers make you feel? Are you glad for having the time and space—a holiday—to allow you to think of these things too?

Now, as this year fades, many of you will see this period as a new beginning. Perhaps you are happy—or rather hopeful—you can start afresh ... seeing this date as a pivotal turning point in which to alter yourself or your surroundings with those so-called resolutions. Come what may, whatever you are considering, try to remember the saying, 'change the things you can, and accept the things you cannot'.

Many factors come into play within this attitude and thought process, none less so than one's faith. How you conduct yourselves, reacting and interacting with your fellow souls is also essential, because this reflects (and resonates), a greater vibration of light and love ... but it can expand disdain, darkness and hate too.

Over the past 365 days, you can contemplate upon many things, none less so than your progress as a human being and a soul. Do you believe you have grown as a person, becoming more confident, glowing, and in doing so, help others and society? Do you now sense you are not so much an individual, but are part of the truth, the way, and the life of all things? Remember, I am not your judge and jury here, for you are each your own in this respect.

I state such things to new readers of this text and to someone who, over many months, has read and digested these words from, through and to their heart. Well, do you behave differently? Are your opinions the same? Can you accept who, what and why you exist, and if so, perhaps others see a real or even subtle change within you now.

In fact, some people may not believe you are different in any way, shape, or form. On the other hand, perhaps friends and family have also altered or even display new attitudes towards you now. Overall, you might deem these as outside viewpoints and thoughts, but can they be discounted or ignored?

No one should ever try to make you feel guilty, ashamed, or think that whatever faith or religion you follow is in any way questionable. Remember, if it only reflects peace and kindness, then this qualifies as being truthful.

Indeed, what resonates within may be true to one and not another. However, should your own conduct exude love, then the opinions, reasoning, and any outside influence cannot dilute it. For this very reason, your own truth matters, and no one else's.

Also, when an individual or some group of people, and even a government or country, tries to enforce or coerce even one soul to behave or enact what they are not, then conflict and dissatisfaction will always take hold. This spreads like a cancer, with negative energy and stress causing a disease amongst men. But do not fear (as I continually explain to you), because light and love are both in and around you... and is you too.

This is a fact, not fiction, and above all things. Hence, do not despair when across your world you bear witness, hear, or experience what you may call abhorrent or horrific behaviour by a person, group, or nation. Should you now ask or think, "How (or why) can I say this to you?" ... I would simply reply, "I do not make mistakes." Is this arrogance ... soulless or shameless? Would this suggest there is an overall 'plan' for you and the entire world, which must come in a set sequence in order to be happy?

Many people imagine you are all actors on the stage of life. Well, if so, what expressions do you see upon it at this point of your lives ... and who raises or lowers the curtain? (Consider the consonants of the word 'curtain', and perhaps contemplate 'creation' here instead).

In the performance itself, are you displaying the truth and true you, or, like a chameleon; forever disguising and changing yourself? Should the latter be the case, is this for your own or for someone else's so-called benefit? Please realise, whether young or old, there is a real part for you to play, as this is not a game or child's toy to behold.

Understand you yourselves choose and receive a role, but do not worry or concern yourself whether it is the main lead. In fact, this comparison with your life (containing one's experiences and expression), means you do not need the most lines to say ... to impact or influence others.

Indeed, your own appearance in this world can state more than a thousand words or 'scenes'. Your heart and smile can inspire and shine far greater than those who appear to be in the limelight, and who get what some call 'false' glory. You do not need a medal or an Oscar for me to recognize your true worth. In all walks of life, the simple act of one's performance is sufficient ... if you try your utmost to become the best person and soul you can be.

While you are living your life, suppress the ego, because you do not need approval or applause to be needed or satisfied. All these feelings are within you. By reflecting upon them, you will understand your real self beyond all doubt. You are your own witness, viewing the truth (both inside and out), and therefore able to realise who and what I am, too.

It is this acceptance, which will lead you to your goal and fulfilment ... your ascension and destiny. You move beyond the impermanent appearance of being 'human', to shine like the 'Son'.

I will now refocus your mind and return your thoughts to the start of this lesson. With the New Year approaching in most hearts and homes across the 'earth-plane', will you rejoice and symbolically turn over a new leaf and life? Can this be a fresh chapter and a new beginning for each one of you?

Please appreciate, the slightest positive alteration in your character, personality and conduct can change so much around you, and even though trepidation and anxiety may remain, everyone can radiate and share in the love of you all. Therefore, by linking hands with your family, friends, neighbours, colleagues, or strangers, or even those who need your forgiveness, the New Year can be celebrated with sincere hope and joy for all.

Likewise, when those who come to the end of their earthbound existence, (having completed and played their part), they may stand together arm in arm to display unity and peace like a victory bestowed. This will lead to spontaneous applause and congratulations from soul to soul, expanding love and light beyond any theatre of dreams.

As a result, accept the way you live, work, and play as you are right now, or become stronger, brighter, more loving, and forgiving. Do what you will and will what you do, because any restrictions and boundaries are self-imposed and set.

Believe you are strong; stronger than you can ever possibly imagine, because no four walls, no false mind, nor any delusion or confusion can contain your truth, essence, and soul. You are not trapped, caged, or controlled, so do not think of such in a material sense, as your 'self' is already free to soar as high and far as your will allows you. If you are ever in doubt, or think you are alone, turn 'within'.

Be 'still' to feel the love, and you will know and trust me, for inside you ... 'I am I'. Understand that the acceptance of yourself—and me—shall light the way ... beyond your New Year and forever and a day. Truly, we are one and eternal, and this the real cause for celebration. Amen.

LESSON 17:
EXPRESSION

Welcome! Please become 'still', so you may listen and learn and bear witness to the text on this page, and share the light, which shines through and from you all, too.

Regarding today's lesson, I understand many of you find it difficult to express yourselves, or 'see' what others portray in their thoughts and words and deeds. This can seem strange to those elementals and other life forces that surround and watch over you all ... because with such beauty and radiance of light within you, one should naturally radiate from the heart.

However, because of lifestyle, beliefs, conduct, and appearance, not only may these ethereal beings misunderstand you; people even become confused with each other! One must realize then, most of this confusion stems from the inability to say what you feel, think, or want to do. This is a denial of self-expression, often caused by the fear of rejection, or concern for your own (or someone else's) wellbeing.

I will never say do not care for others or stop worrying about another's feelings in your daily lives ...but much of this 'holding back' contains negative traits that reflect towards your inner self. These can make you unwell, feel rundown, or worse still, trigger illness or disease, which is the effect following the cause.

Therefore, what can one do? How should you conduct yourself, as well as interact with others who are close by, or even on the other side of the world? Well, the answer is to live through truth ... whatever your emotions, as your divine essence, need to prevail.

In doing so, may this be with kindness, honesty, compassion, and love, then the energy fields within and around your physical, mental, emotional, and ethereal bodies, will all spiral and dance like seeds blowing upon a breeze, to shine more brightly than the stars above you.

The benefits of letting others see the real you are immense, because not only does it enable you to reveal your true 'self', but those who also witness and sense this experience become enlightened too. In fact, your expression of whom, what and why you exist as a male or female, with different colour skin, religious and physical persuasions (and so on and so forth), all form part of your own soul's picture, which is a piece of the universal jigsaw of our 'one' heart.

The importance here is not deny yourself and the truth, which lies inside you. Do not to be misguided by other forms of persuasion, particularly by those who wish or try to impose their will upon you, leading to delusion and the inherent gift of self-expression becoming hidden or withdrawn. This would resemble a flower kept inside a darkened room, its radiance confined ... to eventually wither, fade, and die.

Please realise some of what I convey to you can become self-inflicted ... if your soul wishes to deny its own wellbeing, or still tries to disrupt or hurt others who are linked by any of the four 'bodies' I mentioned earlier. These acts are often despised ... not only by the individual but also by family or friends too. However, each soul can prevent such instances and unhappiness by sharing and sending out love, kindness, and compassion.

Remember, it is not appropriate for anyone to judge another person but try lending a helping hand at all times. Who knows whether the favour or help one gives may be returned by a stranger in one, ten or fifty years from now, or even on another vibration level of existence if truth and balance play its part? Once again, the choice is yours and yours alone, in every aspect of your life.

So then, let me ask you, how do you express yourself? Do you explain and talk, or do you utilise the physical, sending out information and signals through your body language? Both can be meaningful, though, as stated earlier, it is quite easy for those who draw close upon the various planes of existence to become confused or mystified by what is often said or done.

This is because true expression comes only from within you, and this guiding light is a beacon, strengthening your character and personality, and through these attributes, the viewer, listener, or the participant of a joint activity will realise this.

One ought to consider, that to rely upon words alone (to either explain or show their love), will fail in breaking down those physical, emotional, mental, or social barriers, which each soul has erected or inflicted upon themselves over the millennia. In addition, speech itself is too diverse, with many negative traits. What is nectar to one could bring distress and become poisonous to another.

Therefore, in silence, you will find the truth, and the spiritual seeker knows that through their experience comes the real expression of our love as 'one'. By feeling and acknowledging this connection each day, your faith can grow stronger, and this will enable you to express yourself in your true light.

Appreciate for too long now, the obscurity of illusion, which befalls the impermanent world, has dimmed human being's illumination. However, every person can take a step—no matter how small—to emerge from the darkness and shadow of doubt. Then, as one moves forward, your life and the journey becomes easier to understand, and enables you to comprehend more of what and why you are as you are.

Please realise, only the individual can make their own commitment to embark upon the journey to eternal bliss and peace. Think of this as a voyage, a continued quest, and a mission you cannot leave into the hands of another which is your own burden, and yet your joy, your incomprehensible joy.

Not forgetting those who have met their goal and therefore ascended, because their light shines love unto all. They see, sense, and know you, and hear your hearts, souls, and minds as one. They aid you in immense and vastly different ways, expressing themselves in helping and encouraging and supporting you, especially through your assumed troubled times.

Love is the ultimate expression they give so freely to you all. You are not their mother, father, sister, or brother, or in fact any other person you would care to imagine, for they, you and we are all one family. Unconditional is their love, it is a sacrifice, and their humility echoes both far and wide, resonating on many vibration levels.

Conversely, those who lie in the gutter will see and experience me through the strangers who offer them food, water, and comforts. In contrast, people who live in opulence and decadence will come to recognize me through their own expression too, if they can discover and acknowledge this in their hearts.

Make no mistake; I do not judge any of you by colour, creed, or whatever possessions you have accumulated in this world upon the 'earth-plane'. In addition, whether meek and poor or rich and famous, no one is more, or any less worthy, of my grace.

You all emanate from my heart, and only when humanity as whole expresses love through their own hearts can total self-realization be fulfilled. Therefore, trust in me during all your endeavours ... and live in the knowledge your beautiful light can never be extinguished, for you are the expression and truth of me. Amen.

LESSON 18:
CREATIVITY LEADS TO FREEDOM AND EXPRESSION

As you sit, pondering over this new message and lesson, your whole demeanour slows down as you become 'still'. Your heart rate has dropped, your breathing more relaxed, and as you gaze upon the clouds through the window, time itself seems to drift by. By allowing yourself these moments of peace and contemplation, your physical body will benefit from the rest and relaxation (after the toils of the day). Your mind will also become untangled from one's thoughts that bind and trap an individual into the daily existence of 'living'.

Countless souls wish to develop and grow into something more, and often ask or pray to free their mind, "Please God, help me find the freedom I need" or "Dear God … please release me from what is happening." Perhaps circumstances take hold and grip their life like a vice—or affect their family's situation—regarding work, home, or even monetary aspects of their well-being.

Understand these important issues, where you believe you need a desired outcome, are much easier to achieve than people realise. Many queries or quandaries will captivate or confuse, but all you need to do is to release the senses you possess in order to 'free' the mind. This is because each sense can lead to desire, and these will pursue you in their many forms, resulting in attachment, which controls your thoughts and actions. However, by letting these go, you untie the bonds, which prevent your true pursuit of stillness and creativity.

Your light then radiates and expands, and not only are you able to bear witness to truth but your true self shines … recognized by those on the 'earth-plane' and in the planes of vibration and ether. Removing ego and any self-desire brings peace with whom you are and what you do. Imagine someone who walks into a room full of people and everyone bears witness to their presence, because deep down they illuminate and radiate both happiness and contentment.

Of course, many sages, devotees, saints, and disciples over the centuries would automatically appear this way, and so the gift of peace (to help you recognize the same freedom), is within your own grasp. The process will become easier, second nature if you like, but first you must wish for it inside yourself, and by acknowledging this true need, you are halfway there. Please remember, denying this only fuels the illusion and confusion, which will then make your life feel you are being pulled in different directions, with much worry and stress.

I will now assume you are becoming 'still' regularly, and therefore many beautiful things can be set in motion. Some will remain hidden and may not appear to come into view for many of your earth years, while others will hit you like a thunderbolt, straight out of the blue. (Do not fear that they will hurt you, for I do not mean this).

Understand there are spiritual beings, guides and angels watching over you all, too. They assist in karmic actions, as well as observing the cause and effect within and all around you, in order for opportunities to be created through acknowledgement and progress. New 'doors' can be opened, and they can guide people and situations in your direction to help and assist you in your spiritual education and path.

You are experiencing this, when you realise something in your life has just fallen right into place and you cannot believe your luck! You receive a job offer or you pass a test or exam. Perhaps you were successful in buying a house to turn into your dream home, or you become a parent for the first time. These are only examples, and I am not saying these things occur without your effort too ... if you let go and simply 'be', then dreams come true, and miracles happen.

When you are 'still' within the silence, your inner child becomes free, you loosen those constraints created by your own mind, and nothing can hold you back. In fact, there is no place in existence where you cannot go, or soul whose presence you cannot be feel or see. You can achieve anything, within peace and truth.

Over time, your light becomes brighter, and creativity inside you expands and develops, too. The abilities you possess (from the power which is you and I) are enhanced; and will grow further in so many ways. Remember, all spiritual gifts are already inside each one of you, and when you are ready to live in love, share love, and be love, it returns tenfold to you.

Yet, this is not the reason you embark upon your new quest for liberation and bliss, and I reiterate this because I acknowledge everything ... though most do not recognise these methods used. In terms of action and reaction, I will not preside over you all to observe and weigh the scales of justice and injustice. These things are already in place for you to work through and balance ... as your lives, karma, and souls have decreed.

That said, every single human being could assist in global ascension towards fulfilment and bliss. Each person can link hands and hearts with his neighbour, their community, and their country ... and all nations can realise they are one united family.

All must comprehend and appreciate that freedom is not something you need to aspire to, because 'within' you are already free. The cell or prison of your embodiment is unreal and false. You are the key to open the lock of those imaginary doors, which contain your dreams and wishes at bay.

As this passage now draws to a close, I request you are true to yourself, and within this truth, you will be true to each other. In the quietness and stillness, you will sense and know me with all your heart, for I hold you in my arms, and I will let none of you go.

Every life, soul, atom, particle, chemical and aspect of creation, I am. I express myself through your lives. I ask you to fulfil yourselves in truth, in love, and in light ... so from this day forth, you can truly express yourself in your life, too. Amen.

LESSON 19:
FREEDOM AND POWER

So, who is free? I ask this straight away, because it is important for everyone who reads or hears this 'lesson' to think about what freedom means. Some may state this is an obvious question-and-answer scenario, but you will need to dig far deeper into your mind and heart to understand the truth.

In reality, everything is simple, because love resonates to and from itself in all places. The answer, therefore, hangs over every soul, either as a question or an exclamation mark ... depending upon the acceptance of the light within you.

On the surface, one might deem any form of life not trapped or caged as being 'free', and in one sense, this is true regarding the 'earth-plane' and the way you live. However, the real issue is not in the freedom where you live now, but where your soul's destiny lies ... which I will explain in more detail shortly.

For all in your current embodiments, you are actually living a life of false bondage, an attachment you have contributed to yourselves. If this were not the case, then you would not be reading or hearing these words. Likewise, by your own hand and choice, one's karma and right action has decreed your spiritual education must continue to use such knowledge, and then, through 'experience' ... gain wisdom.

Remember, there is the unique opportunity to attain self-realization and liberation of this age. So, at what point do you comprehend this and believe in who, what, and why you are? As basic freedom is choice, the onus is upon the individual to move forward and become a brighter and lighter being of love.

Throughout the process called life that you travel upon, help, guidance, and encouragement will be given as your needs arise. These can evolve from the meeting of like-minded hearts and souls, which offer new windows of clarity and insight. This enables the seeker of truth to feel and experience greater knowledge and understanding, and this is self-perpetuating. (Think of a small snowball, which rolls down a steep slope. It will gain momentum and grow).

During your experiences, your growth can continue, stay the same (depending on your inner strength and conviction), or even fade and slip away, as if melted by the heat from the Sun. This does not happen very often, but when it does, exterior forces and negativity (sometimes not karmic), pick away at the truth ... trying to dismantle or bring disharmony to those who may be 'sitting on the fence' (with more than a little doubt), which then leads to greater confusion both within and out.

In contrast, by passionately believing and keeping faith in yourself, you will have more than enough attributes to realise the right from wrong in your work, rest, and play. If you are weak, pray for strength. If you are strong, pray that you may help those who are fragile and need encouragement too.

These prayers from your heart, or even those thoughts of the mind, enable you to comprehend the choice and answer regarding the initial question I asked you earlier. Therefore, if you were to contemplate or meditate upon freedom, you would understand its meaning and importance too.

Now, try to imagine someone incarcerated, and his or her 'physical' choices removed. They may not move about, see daylight, or even receive any food or water. Any individual denied these things could believe they are weak, their resolve broken, or perhaps feel their life ebbing away. However, I say to you ... within thy self and body, or even by being aware of such things going on around you, be strong, stronger than you ever thought you could be. You are not alone and never can be, for I am with you in all situations and every event of your life!

Know too, throughout Earth's history, man and animals have been shackled or caged ... restrained for someone's pleasure, or for their skin, fur, and food. This reverts to the beastly traits and negativity deep within the psyche. In time, man will realise any unnecessary and futile actions only bring about death and decay, hate and despair, which have more implications and far-reaching effects than is known to you all at this time.

One must appreciate you are already free, and this is inherent from me. You have the freedom to be whom and what you are, in all situations and places, so you must always determine whether your thoughts, words or deeds are in truth or not. The ability to be kind, generous, and considerate lies within you, which enables you to be a person with true values as a human being, who helps to expand the hand of friendship and heart of love. One can also express these traits through your own creativity, and not walls or bars can contain this asset and real power of you.

On the exterior, someone may even see you as a weak person, who might appear indecisive, fragile, or a pushover, but looks can be deceiving. Your strength is the character of your heart and soul. This is the truest and strongest 'muscle' you can exercise properly to defend negativity. In fact, you are more powerful than you could ever imagine, so who can stop your hopes and dreams? What physical structure can contain your love? Unseen and unheard does not mean you fail to exist!

You are all amazing and yet have faults. However, if you learn from past mistakes, you can reach and fulfil your goal of eternal bliss. The power within you is so vast … if only you realise, accept, and then understand it.

We are one, and therefore, through this connection, you will find the answers and freedom you crave and seek. Your spark and divine essence can become brighter and clearer every day if you wish it, too. In fact, the flame of love and light inside you shall bloom like a flower, and its petals will glisten and shimmer … more beautiful than the stars that shine within the darkest and clearest of nights. Please know that your love is sweeter than nectar and more fragrant than any field of majestic and radiant flowers.

Therefore, by enquiring about 'real' freedom, you will encourage the development of your soul, enriched through your heart. This is a gift that can be shared amongst those you meet—and link up with—upon the various planes of dimensions and time.

Remember, people who live their lives by truth touch many hearts in countless ways. As stated earlier, someone may walk into a room full of people and their presence felt by all, for they illuminate and shine the true energy of love from within their core, so much so, their aura touches even hardened shells.

Such a soul is an example of freedom through expression. But do not become a follower of any 'man', as they still have their own karma to play out, and because you are the disciple and the seeker of your own truth.

In conclusion, it is only 'within' where this teacher resides. Inside, the reality is waiting to be discovered. There, you not only find me but also, you're true 'Self'. Here, you will experience real freedom and power beyond imagination. Indeed, your destiny and goal now await you. Amen.

LESSON 20:
INFINITY

Suddenly you imagine a symbol, a sign of the 'above and below'—perhaps a figure eight—which then leads to an opening, an eternal heavenly gate. In contemplation, thoughts often drift to fate while looking towards the heavens ... dreams of family, a child, or a mate. So, where has this begun, and why does my life struggle when I should be having fun?

These are amongst the many concerns held by the inquirers of truth, who aspire and seek answers from within and out. In fact, people often delve deep into their feelings regarding information from another person, who may then lead them astray, misguide, or even misinterpret what they seek or ask for.

Therefore, the full responsibility and quest for your own knowledge comes from inside you. This is the only perpetual and everlasting source of divinity, which is 'I am I' and 'me'. All else is secondary ... and will take you only so far upon the spiritual path of 'self-realization' and wisdom.

Every book and person can affect you by pushing you further away—or through truth—lead you nearer to me. Comprehend that true education and guidance will resonate inside you, and if your heart feels the connection, follow this. However, should what you read, see, or hear seem awkward, leave it to one side, and a "thanks, but no thanks", will suffice.

The expression of 'as above, so below' contains many connotations for you all, including the perception of 'as in Heaven, so shall it be it on Earth'. Actually, the balance of numerous planes, dimensions and vibration levels is everywhere. Hence, the physical world receives and sends these too. Life force cannot be crushed, burnt, erased, or fade, for this would be taking something permanent and trying to make it disappear, like a magician's trick. This is an illusion, which fools and sways so many people to disbelieve and fear the unknown, too.

In comparison, your heart is the one reality, and my love is the wand that lights the way, weaving and connecting strands of energy to and from you. Therefore, a magical bond between hearts exists, and is too strong to be broken, and only the veil of delusion hides this reality from you.

Like a mist, which rolls down from the mountains and hills of your soul's karma, it sweeps in, disguising the true light. One can gaze upon this, but when unfocused, the reality resembles frosted glass with misshapen images, blurred choices, and goals. To reach your immortality and infinity of bliss, you need to push aside this untruth and wade through the fog of wrong action to be clean and free from the bondage of death and rebirth.

Perhaps you are also experiencing difficult times or challenges, such as health issues, family troubles, financial hardship, or if you are lonely, hungry, or cold, what do you do? Where do you go? Well, grasp that whatever part you play—or stage you find yourself upon—I am the platform, the audience, and the director of all things, but you are not my puppet on a string, either.

Remember, even though people often look for my help only in times of strife, you can 'realise' me through all of your senses (and so much more), and when I experience your joy and laughter, this echoes even louder through me than you can imagine. I state this in case you believe I am impervious to what occurs within your life and heart, but I know you better than you do yourself and comprehend everything taking place.

You may ask, "Why do I sometimes suffer so much? Why do these events happen to me and not to him, her, or them over there? What have I done to deserve this?" Moreover, during true desperation comes the cry, "Where is God?" In fact, these moments are precisely when words are no longer required, for even a single tear shows me the truth of your emotional, physical, or mental pain. So, where do the answers lie?

This query and the outcome (the result), stem from reaction to action and vice versa. Balance includes both the positive and negative, and through the experience itself, which is cause and effect. I do not point a finger, chastise, or hate anyone above or below another, or interfere with what you, yourself, and your karma bring, either.

Try to understand, I am not blind, deaf, or distant to any heart, for I am you and you are me. You are never alone, and only fear makes you seem further away from me, which is untrue. In every situation, you can sense me through truth, so ignore the deception from—and by—the worst fear of all ... death. Realise too, faith in yourself also shows true faith in me.

In addition, attempt to treat all experiences the same, for they lead all to one's growth, and because knowledge and self-realization are the real keys to your spiritual pathway and goal. Be content too, and desire only to reside with me forever. I am here, there, and everywhere; and am always with you, loving you, and aware of every situation in which you find yourself.

Therefore, be kind, courteous, and helpful to all living things. Nurture nature and each other, or even a stranger. Dispense with your inner enemies of anger, jealousy, hatred, ego, and pride. Go with the flow like the tide, and turn within, do not hide. You are all special, all individual characters, yet every soul is 'one', because we are totality.

Be still, and do not fret, worry, or fear, but hold me near. Keep me in your thoughts too, and realise I am below, above and the in-between. So, if you keep love in your heart, then you cannot fail to grasp what I mean. Be true, not blue ... for you are I, and I am eternally you. Therefore, please rest in peace, within love, light, and truth always. Amen.

LESSON 21:
THOUGHTS

Please appreciate, there are many people and countless different beings throughout creation, because life exists upon every dimension and inside vibration energies. Some may live alone (in physical terms only, as my love flows through all things), and they carry on their daily tasks only having to think about themselves.

Within their mind, they act out various scenarios, and subsequently, these thoughts trigger a desire. This starts all kinds of actions, which then activates a resulting function ... cause and effect. In such circumstances, a human, animal, any form of being, or even insects, gives insufficient consideration towards the potential consequences of a single 'thought'. From survival-instincts to self-gratification, and everything else one could think of in-between; all trigger this process.

Consider two elements of 'life', who now confront each other, they could be people, strange beings, animals, or perhaps small parasites. Now imagine they are in a dense jungle, upon a desert plain, or deep within an ocean, and then they attack; hurt or one even kills the other. What thoughts or feelings do you think have taken place? Some may state, "Well, its survival of the fittest" and "instinct", or even say that nature is a law unto itself, but is it? Even at a base level of evolution, a thought has to take place, resulting in 'action'.

Many scientists, philosophers and highly intellectual people through different eras often believed it is only humans who can think, explaining other brains are far too small, and lack intelligence. Appreciate a thought does not develop in the brain, because thought is consciousness, and can originate during sleep and an awakened state. As this is so, even minute micro-biotic creatures try to stay alive. Therefore, what is the difference between these and humankind? Are people more noble, kind, or are they vulnerable?

Comprehend there are fewer differences between beings and elements of life compared with 'man' than one would expect. In reality, the main distinction is in your ability to 'feel' through thoughts and become emotionally linked to their consequences. I bless you all with this inherent gift for the soul, but even though this is precious ... in terms of one's progress, people waste time because of selfishness and greed for what is impermanent upon the 'earth-plane'.

There is much to learn in order to move away from this lifestyle and type of existence. However, by remembering the two simple traits of forgiveness and compassion (which are deep inside you all); they can help to bring a real change. Though having subtle differences, they are the same thing, for they simply lie beside (and within) the same love of both you and I, and this is the basis for all life and creation.

Do not think you are above anyone else, or pigeonhole these qualities as random acts of kindness, unable to display them. Acknowledge they are as inherent inside you as your heart and lungs, and like your physical legs, which provide the ability to move or crawl, carry you forward through the so-called 'good and bad' times as your daily life unfolds.

Okay, earlier we envisaged a scenario of two creatures facing each other. One may live and the other die. Likewise, human beings on all continents cause conflict on both large and small scales. From a neighbourly dispute to different religions trying to co-exist, there seems to be attitudes and thoughts of 'I must win', or continual attempts to exert control over another. Little debate takes place, and more often than not, physical force is used.

One should realise there are no real differences between any of you. All are without division or separation. When this clear and defined notion manifests itself in the heart, it transcends into thought and right action, which ensures a positive outcome. Within this process, forgiveness, and compassion trickle through as love.

When a daughter or son is murdered, a father or mother passes away, a home is destroyed, a livelihood removed, a loved one becomes seriously ill, a pet disappears, or when countless other scenarios are contemplated upon, what do you believe in? What thoughts or images flow in your heart? What type of tear do you shed?

Human beings tend to prioritise everything, including what they own, as well as other people in their lives. Some may feel their pet is more important than a relative, or vice versa. Strangely, some give a greater concern to a materialistic possession than even their own body! In addition, there are those who deem themselves as not being physically 'whole'—missing limbs or a sense of sight—so they would never accept or do this.

In all circumstances, selfishness should change to selflessness, so that a clenched fist becomes an open hand outstretched to help the fallen. Likewise, each of you can turn over a new leaf right now ... not later, nor tomorrow, next week or next year. And physically, you do not need to go anywhere; because you can send love and light to all things in all places ... if you only believe, so, do you?

With sincerity, your love emanates through your heart, and those thoughts of kindness and compassion shall shine like beacons or sparkle like beautiful stars. Rekindled in truth; you will embrace, foster, and share this love and light. You connect, becoming radiant and magical, to be cast upon my breath as stardust, sprinkled across time, space, and all dimensions.

So, what choice or option should you make and take? Well, "Do what you feel and feel what you do" are the same words I have said countless times—to all beings since time immemorial—though all I ask is that you try to become everything you can be.

May your soul fly to new heights and beyond your wildest dreams, to reach your goal; the eternal peace and destiny 'within' me. Remember, everything can reflect your true self.

LOVE ALL ... ALL LOVE.
PEACE FOR ALL ... ALL FOR PEACE.
OPEN HEART ... HEART OPEN.
REACH DIVINITY ... DIVINITY REACHED.

Amen.

LESSON 22:
COMPASSION

"Dear God, please let your truth and light flow through this pen. May words of wisdom bleed from within my heart and through our connection, to bring understanding, hope and guidance, especially to all those who need your help and love at this time." DK.

Today, you overheard two sides to a story: an argument, a debate, and a summary of events. In over-view, this was a situation displeasing many people, shocking some, and yet brought no despair to others. I shall not discuss the incident itself but wish you to convey the thought processes and subtle differences that transpire within the hearts and minds of all.

As mentioned on countless occasions, whether you are awake or asleep, you are all but a reflection of me. In thought and word and deed and in body, mind, and soul, there is no separation or division, and this provides you with the ability to focus on every positive aspect of living and being. It is the choice and so-called 'free will', which therefore dissipates, dilutes, and filters good actions from bad, and the effect from the cause.

If one calls another's action perverse, evil, ungodly, or cowardly, what ought to be realised concerning any event that's witnessed, heard, or indeed took part in can also be the same reflection of what lies within themselves. Strange to some, this may be, but it is important to understand the reality of the potential and actual consequences. Sometimes, those who are not aware of all the facts review the scenario with some sort of divine judgement, but all should remember, do not judge lest ye be judged yourself.

Should someone disagree with your belief system or moral viewpoint, do not be quick to condemn, hate or despise him or her, because you will be unaware of what karma has been balanced or erased. This should not be a difficult aspect to grasp, especially for those embarking upon their own spiritual quest and path for greater knowledge and wisdom of their self and goal.

Please do not believe things occur without meaning either, for nothing does or ever will. I recognize all things, and everything exists in their rightful place for the right outcome and overall good of love and light.

Consider blindness, for though one cannot see with physical eyes, you can still bear witness to the truth within. Therefore, do not dwell upon negative outcomes, but continue to have confidence in yourself and your actions of right over wrong. By doing so, your faith in me grows stronger, and you will lose fear of anyone or anything.

In all scenarios, your essence cannot be diminished or taken away. As I keep reiterating, I am you and you are me. We are whole, complete, so only the false impression and illusions of the physical world you temporarily live upon makes some people think otherwise.

In fact, you may well come across situations where not only your beliefs or thoughts are disagreed with. When these occur, one simple process lies within your capabilities, and enables you to overcome them all ... compassion.

Delving deeper, who is more compassionate, the male or the female? And is the strength and bond (or perhaps the ache and pain) of love felt more by one than the other? Realise in all beings, this trait, quality, and the emotions tugging upon heartstrings are not from a master puppeteer above but lie deep within your own core.

In contrast, when ugliness rears its head, darkness and negativity is picking and stabbing your consciousness, how do you react? What should you say or do? This may seem or sound complicated, but it is not. When you live truthfully, life is simplicity itself, so the only answer is love. Remember, through love flows compassion, and vice versa.

Some actions of others can appear to be so distasteful you cannot bear to speak or look at them. How do you know they are not physically, mentally, or emotionally ill? Just flip the coin and ask about the moral judgement of your own behaviour today, yesterday, last month or last year. Are there not many actions or thoughts that you yourself would have done differently, and changed upon reflection? Please understand, until you strive and reach your goal, try to be the best human being you can be.

Whether you are a mother, father, child, brother, sister, carer, employee, manager, director, an orphan, an immigrant, politician, a King or Queen (and so on and so forth), these 'clothes' you were born into make no difference to me, for you should all act and wear them with justice and fortitude.

In all endeavours, compassion should prevail, whether to your fellow man or the creatures and animals inhabiting the 'earth-plane' too. The colour of your skin and the language you speak bear absolutely no relevance in the heart and heart's centre. True love is without barriers, in any way and shape or form.

Where help is required—perhaps someone or something is in distress or ill health—they do not care or think of looks and appearance, one's colour, voice, religious beliefs, or background. Compassion strives not in the clenched fist or raised tone, but in an outstretched helping hand, whether by face or even over the telephone!

One can be compassionate through thought and prayer, or even a smile to show you care. By supporting others and the society in which you live, you come out of your shell to no longer hide. Perhaps one day, you yourself will need someone to guide or help you along your way and journey. Therefore, compassion in its many forms can illuminate and shine both to and from you, if you will, but hold on to truth and love inside your heart.

Appreciate your real character resides within every word, thought and deed, as they all reflect and resonate love (or lack of). Common phrases like, "So you sow, so shall you reap" and "What goes around comes around" ring true. I am not asking you to be a saint, but request you take control of your life in order to be your true self.

Do not waste time, energy, or money on the impermanent, but seek the truth in all you do. Dismiss desire, want and greed, as they will slow you down in your pursuit of righteousness and the glory of yourself. However, you ought to take pleasure in your life because you are 'alive', and so all things, as long as they do not hurt you (or another), physically, mentally, emotionally, or spiritually, should be enjoyed!

You are all one family of love and light, so whether you are on different sides of the world; try to think about and aid others. By being compassionate in all that is said and done, there will remain an everlasting memory of the 'one'. Everything is connected. So, no matter how unique or diverse someone or something appears, you will still see me, and therefore yourself.

You are love and love is you,
Know the truth, as truth knows you.
Friends in compassion, brings compassionate friends,
So change today and set a trend.

Whether thick, thin, fat, or small,
Head not in clouds, hearts free, not bound.
Glory to me, my glory to you,
We are one forever, so live in truth.

Amen.

LESSON 23:

DEEDS NOT WORDS

Since time immemorial, countless people upon the 'earth-plane' have guided their thoughts towards deities, gods, and even the Sun and Moon. In fact, many believed they could send their love, wishes, and desires to something or someone would bring divine inspiration, protection, or guidance to help them in their lives. However, anything emanating solely from the mind only dissipates upon and within the ether.

Please understand, only prayers sent through and from the heart will gather enough momentum and strength to reach out and reverberate from me. Governed by love and light, they attain the required outcome for both progress and understanding.

It is important for the individual and the masses to grasp and comprehend this clearly defined difference, with a conviction to conclude and meet the one goal which determines your soul's continued journey into eternity.

Therefore, whilst so many of you practice meditation, say your decrees, and send prayers to me every day (which are all vital for the wellbeing of yourself and all elements of life), they are only parts of what make you whole ... combined with your persona and character. In light of this, you can now leap forward and grasp the wider picture of whom, what, and the why of your daily lives in thought, word, and deed.

You may remember the simple analogy, 'actions speak louder than words', which is something to be considered today. This is because so many people think they do enough by requesting or offering support through the 'spoken word', but what needs to take place is personal involvement, for the 'deed' takes precedent over what you speak.

Indeed, hands that help are holier than lips that pray. While prayers are vibrations of love flowing across time and dimension, the physical body, which contains both your heart and mine, carries out the process itself. Reflect upon this for a moment, and establish the truth deep inside of you, as it beholds you all.

Countless opportunities—to help different forms of life—come and go throughout your journey. These are utilised or even missed altogether. In essence, I can produce these openings for you, but you also create the same through the decisions you make, too.

When these materialize and you enact upon them, the energy of love vibrates and dances, like diamonds and crystals reflecting sunlight all around you, as well as during the event (or action) taking place. This is true in all places of existence, and cannot be diluted or defused by negativity, darkness or hate. Love knows no bounds. It is forever seen and felt by hearts not blinded or encased by illusion. Comprehend that love seeks no reward, for love is its own reward.

Love and light are so beautiful and simple in its entirety and no matter what you carry out in peace and truth, the same effect always takes place. So, whether you help a struggling insect, fallen over on its back, or travel across the street, town, country or even the other side of the globe to aid the poor and hungry, you sense the resonance within and out.

People often prioritise insects, animals, people, and the world into their own pigeonholes, each having their fate or lives held by an individual or religious belief system. But only when the penny finally drops to believe we are all one with no diversity and separateness can humankind ascend as one 'body', together in unity.

Currently, decades of time upon the Earth pass by, with few attaining their ascension and eternity in me. If more people had opened their minds and hearts throughout previous incarnations, acting Godlier in everything said and done, then billions of souls would be within the permanent state of love, instead of the impermanent world and physical vibration.

Please do not panic or fret yourself into an early grave, though, as all you need to change is right inside you. All you need to do is look, but more importantly understand, the openings and opportunities in your daily life. Do not strain and think you cannot see them. Focus on what you think, say, and do ... then, like pieces of a jigsaw connecting, you will see the true picture in all its glory.

Please try not to think of the worst in people, especially when they do you harm or are angry with you. By trying your best in all you do, self-realization is inevitable. I appreciate some people imagine the world as being beyond help, and hence cannot realise the dream, but it is not, and never will be, out of your grasp. That said, if your 'helping hand' was right in front of you, would you reach and take it?

By now, you can fully comprehend I am within and beside you, so you are never alone. Together, we are one, and by opening your heart, you will return to where you really belong. Therefore, do not worry when things seem to go wrong in your life, or if you fall down, say you cannot get back up again, because such a hurdle could be the last one you ever need to overcome.

Should your life seem unbearable, think of me, trust me, and remember your faith in me. Through having confidence in yourself, everything is easier to bear, and I will carry you. I urge you, please put effort into being the best person and being you can be, and follow, speak, and enact the truth, as we have discussed all along.

All are free ... though most live through bondage, because of their own 'false' self, which deceives them. In your heart, start to trust and believe the advice and guidance from many sources which will come into your life ... some are right for you all, while others are only for those who have balanced their karma. Take only on board what feels right for you as an individual, because if it rings true, you will resonate 'within', and act upon this to grow, and help others too.

Sow the seeds of love and let the deeds of action and truth multiply far beyond the walls of your home. The internal and external barriers will fall, enabling more people to hear your call ... then they will realise love and light is everything. You are all eternal, and I see, know, and love you ... remember. Amen.

LESSON 24:
'TRUST AND FAITH'

Welcome again to 'stillness' and some contemplation time, enabling you to reflect and clear out those thoughts, which inhibit clarity and will soon bring you peace. The working day is done, so be still and rejoice in the calmness of your true self, for you and I are 'one'.

Understand my love washes over you all, but many do not sense, or become 'still', in order to appreciate and grow within it. Everyone will do so, but not until they realise who, what, and why they are a spark of divinity.

Tonight, you can now place your earthly existence on pause, to let light and truth rain in. This will cleanse any doubts, fears and misapprehensions occurring during your day, so do not concern yourself with minor ills or worries, for these are trivial when all is said and done.

Remember, these only take place because you are being 'tested' by 'spirit', to establish one's inherent code of conduct, and whether the individual or the masses can prevail and 'rise above it'. Indeed, as I bear witness to the reaction of such things, this makes perfect sense.

Therefore, it is best to avoid negativity, and those who are unable to express or share the love in their heart, too. You can achieve this diplomatically, without a blank refusal or curse from the tongue. And, if you live by the truth inside you, recognising ill-fated paths and actions becomes second nature.

Remember, being positive also attracts the same where spiritual education and guidance is concerned. However, the expression 'opposites attract' is only true of the physical and impermanent world in which your embodiment lives at this time.

So now I ask you, do you trust in how you act and think? Do you follow your intuition and those 'gut' feelings? If you do, you are acknowledging the unbreakable bond connecting all creation. Please realise, when you place this trust in me, there is no fear. Living without fear brings you peace. Within peace, you find bliss, and in this state of being, your true 'self' shines like a supernova, with magical stardust spiralling and spinning in all directions. In reality, these words cannot express or do justice to such beauty.

In addition, many opportunities throughout your life will come and go, so grasp those that ring true and resonate inside you. When you engage tasks with, by, and through truth, then nothing is impossible to achieve. Only the limits you set or propose to yourselves can prevent the goal of attaining ascension.

Therefore, by trusting in all you truly are, you can reach far beyond what you can or cannot see. Dismiss those false limitations and boundaries, erected only by the insecurities of an illusionary mind. Push these aside with your love, to trust me to give and help you with what you need and require, not in what you think you want and desire.

Remember, you do not need to travel far from your home or disappear deep into a forest to discover me. Finding me is easy, because I am already within and outside of you … as I am all things. In fact, I am the stars at night, shining light through the darkness. I am every leaf and rock. I am earth, fire, water, and air. I am the wind brushing against your face. I am the peace and tranquillity you crave. All these I am, and you are too … no separation or division, only oneness in all.

However, people's thoughts of doubt and despair can still linger both on the 'earth-plane' and upon many vibration levels of energy. "How can I believe? What proof can you provide for me? Why do you let so many lives suffer in pain or anguish?" Please appreciate, I am not blind to any heart that aches or breaks, for I bear witness, sense, and live through them all.

You can wash away your ills and concerns in an instant, but you would not learn or grow. Upon a soul level, mortal man cannot achieve or ease their karmic imbalance this way, so faith is the power to guide and carry you throughout 'life', and its seemingly impossible burdens of work, family, and your general well-being within society. However, many religions from scores of nations use this gift without discernment, and then faith resembles a byword or phrase to indoctrinate hearts and minds.

I am not stating people should throw away any aspect of a religion or cultural inheritance they have grown to know, and one should not consider or decree a life more sacred than someone or something else's is. Considering this, who and what should you believe in? Does your current thought process and belief system enable you to be who you are deep within?

Now, I do not wish to antagonise or offend any being or life, but only the truth (and its reflection) can make another place or person feel this way. Rather this; believe me and so believe in yourself, because true faith in love and light is so magnificent, powerful, beautiful, and amazing, and has no bounds. 'Faith can move mountains' is a saying known too many, but how deep lays this truth, buried inside your hearts over the centuries and eons of time?

My message from this day forth is for you to dig deep into your spiritual core, to grasp and behold this golden nugget. Keep its truth and power close to you each minute of every day. It will never let you down, for as you search and pray, and through your actions, words, and deeds of love, I will polish and smooth the rough edges of your soul's experiences.

So, please have faith in me. Never doubt me, for I do not place doubt in you. My strength will be your strength. My love is your love, and my light is your light. You will shine eternally within me, and your divinity shall remain forever. Show all whom you meet the truth inside you and become a guiding hand to those who doubt or fear, living without faith, even in themselves.

For those who are still unsure, I request a leap of faith does not require you to risk your health (or those of your loved ones), or anything at all to do with your well-being. It is a gap and space, which only appears to exist between you and me. This is unreal, because my love for you is an eternal bridge, which cannot ever crumble. Therefore, seek me by taking just one small step upon it; for I promise you, I will carry you forever into everlasting bliss. Amen.

LESSON 25:

TRUST IN YOU AND ME

I am here and know your thoughts even before you have perceived them yourself. You wonder about the content and subject of this lesson, and think I might disconnect you in some way, or whether you are truly prepared 'within'. Do not worry, fret or be concerned, though, just trust in you and me.

Throughout your daily life—from the moment you awake until your head lies down to sleep again—many choices and tasks become filled with anxiety and fear. Please understand, you can remove these negative traits in an instant, but only if you let the trust, I speak of, enter the core of your heart.

By trusting your own (and in another's) actions, you will ease many disturbances from your mind, but if left unchecked, these afflictions can lead to stress, ill health, disease, and decay of the body. These, in turn, will affect you on further levels, such as the emotional and spiritual 'bodies' that you possess. These may trap you within a circle of questions and doubt, and constantly make you wonder over the outcome in all areas of your life.

What I mean is, instead of letting go and becoming free from the decision or action involved or taken, you will always think whether you have done the right thing, like "What will happen if …" or "If only I had …" and so on and so forth. If you cannot let go of something, or are afraid of a consequence, trust cannot exist, and the effect will follow cause.

So then … who, what, and where would you be comfortable in releasing any concern or worries? Is it within your own home, or perhaps in the presence of family and friends? Well, please realise your heart is wiser than you think, and knows when to trust. Like a mirror, its reflection will become true and wash over you.

The question remains about the level of trust you can give, whether to or from yourself. Material elements (which include possessions) should not enter the equation, for they are impermanent and of no real value where spiritual education is concerned.

Indeed, you may strive to own all manner of items, such as a car, house, furniture, televisions … citing how hard you have worked to acquire them, and believe they are yours, when all along, they are but transitory and fleeting pleasures. I am not saying one cannot be successful, or live in a warm, comfortable home with so-called mod cons, but I request you contemplate upon the meaning of these within your life.

I am not stating you give up any of your comforts, or even the well-being and security for your family, but ask you to re-think and re-prioritize what is beside or within you, so your outlook (of what you sense and feel both inside and out), can change for the better. Do you trust your feelings and thoughts, or does mistrust cast a constant shadow upon you? This question not only falls upon the individual but also the many.

Of course, as you live your life, you will connect with countless people. Therein lies the fear they will always let you down. In not being able to trust someone, you become like a caged bird, forever facing bars in all directions, which not only prevent you from taking flight beyond the 'self' but also to me.

By its own premise, those missed opportunities to shine and grow—because of the illusionary fear—will only make you seem worse, and even when the cage door is open, and freedom beckons, you stand upon the threshold to immortality, but still you wait. Yes indeed, you wait and wait and wait, as if requiring someone or something to pronounce or state, "Go on then, you're free. Come this way, come to me."

Appreciate that through all your experiences, and within the structure of any religion, I will not do this. One may think I am contradicting myself because my helping hand is only a heartbeat away, but you must first recognize it, and then take steps towards me (and real bliss) yourself. Just as a child takes their first baby step, in terms of spiritual education, this action is its equivalent. By developing this inside you, one's confidence and trust will soar in me, too.

Eventually the bird will fly, majestically soaring higher and higher, reaching places beyond dreams. I am your other wing to support and help you do this, and together we can achieve everything you desire in the name of truth, love, and light. However, there will still be testing times during your embodiment, all because your trust can be misplaced or abused.

I state, do not despair when such things trouble your heart and mind, but let them wash over you. Refrain from taking the bait and becoming entangled in the false communications and actions of others. In these circumstances and occasions, it is better to rise above the disruption and any inconvenience someone or something has caused you. This will ensure you focus and re-concentrate upon the truth, and be able to hold your head up high, displaying true human values in all their glory. Think of these annoying moments as minor inconveniences and do not make the proverbial 'mountain out of a molehill'.

Remember, karma and balance always prevail, and in time, one can see their own road clearly ahead. In your life, you will sense what feels right or wrong in thought, word and deed, and your intuition plays a big part of this. This is also a link to the truth, which resonates inside you.

People can become very astute this way, and after a while, this becomes second nature to them. As I have said and discussed before, everyone has the attributes and abilities inside of them to 'succeed' in life. You only need to believe this to believe in yourself ... and then you can believe in me.

Even though 'trust' is a small word, its definition can be as complicated or as simple as one may wish to make it. You can dismiss the idea altogether or take those first 'baby' steps towards joy, peace, and bliss, in the knowledge a helping hand is standing by, lest you fall upon your knees.

Remember, I am within and with you at all times, so I am here, there, and everywhere to help and support you in your endeavours and tasks upon the enlightened road and journey. By taking a step through, to, and with me, your life will change forever! Trusting in me (and yourself), are certainties, for just as the Sun rises to a new dawn each day, I will illuminate your pathway ahead ... with every breath you take. Amen.

LESSON 26:
FROM 'CHILDHOOD' TO 'ADULTHOOD'

Welcome to another 'lesson', and though we have briefly discussed and gone through different periods of your life before, today is not just be about the physical aspect of one's progress, but also the emotional and spiritual development of your being.

So, where do I begin? Most will say, "At the beginning of course", but I would reply, "When was this?" This is because you were never really 'born' (other than into your past and/or current physical embodiments), and so this does not actually apply at all. We are one, and separation or division never enter the equation.

However, because of your soul's development and history of action or karma, there has always been a start, a beginning, or a birth in order to progress and understand who and what you are. More importantly, this enables you to grow and achieve the 'goal', which is the self-realization and liberation of your soul.

To become permanent from the impermanent, you freely undertake the quest for fulfilment and bliss. In relation to the physical, you may not comprehend this until you develop further, passing through the various stages of life.

I easily signposted these as birth, childhood, adolescence, adulthood, and retirement. Imagine and compare your true self as a container, and within it, golden nuggets stacked upon each other. Understand these layers inside are the evolution of your being, which represents your character and appearance, as well as the emotional, mental, and spiritual aspects of 'within'.

Please realise the defining moment of your first cry occurs when you comprehend your rebirth into the impermanent physical world. On the 'earth-plane', a doctor, nurse or midwife may seem to be the instigator ... 'in order—they say—to clear the airways', but this is just cause and effect taking place.

Therefore, you are re-born once more, and no one knows within your karma whether this is only for a minute, a day, or a year ... perhaps even threescore and ten. Well, time is irrelevant, and one's birth could be for your own purposes, or for the benefit in aiding those who are around you, as a group or even soul families also play their part. This may seem far-fetched to some, but within a previous lifetime, you may have even been a next of kin to your current siblings.

The important thing to appreciate here is your debt to your birth mother, which you can never repay. While it is possible to clear all earthly debts, there must always be gratitude towards your mother who carried you. In fact, all actions towards your parents should be respectful, and these should form part of your own human values.

Throughout childhood and adolescence, you are learning and growing upon many levels, through your experiences, actions, and thoughts, which can be positive or negative. One's education also plays a major role in personal responsibility and the development of your character. Some find they are quick learners, whilst others maybe slow, but in trying to be the best you can be, under-achievement or unfulfilled potential does not exist.

The important issue here is to do with regrets. How many people will look upon those missed opportunities to make changes throughout their life, including their early years of schooling? Incomplete dreams and aspirations can haunt a person, for when you age, people often state, "I wish I'd tried harder, or done this or that."

In contrast, there are those with little or even no academic background, who become celebrities or world famous, but do not be confused here, because karmic balancing may be the reasons behind what people call success or failure. The secret is to accept the highs and lows, the triumphs and defeats, the praise or criticism in equal measure. Do not fret, fear, or become excited about what you deem as sad or happy times, as this only wastes energy on 'feelings' which are transparent and translucent.

Be able to hold your head high; not with ego or pride, but in the knowledge your self-esteem and good character are worth your weight in 'spiritual gold'. Realise you can be rich as a king within; while the exterior 'you' that people view (with closed hearts), could be one of paupers. Remember, physical appearance can be deceptive, but when you listen to what resonates inside you, you find the truth. In fact, this will guide you every day as your body ages, and when the weeks, months and years seem to pass by in no time at all.

Please realise too, reaching 'adulthood' does not mean maturity, of course. Many who reach a great age still make petty remarks and do foolish actions; only to lament what they had said and done, or not … as the case may be! Ideally, when you get older, your emotions and thoughts should become more flexible, tolerant, and adaptable to those around you, no matter what their misgivings.

Through your later years, if your efforts and work have come to fruition, you might be able to help people in many other ways. You do not need to own a mansion to think you can finally help other people or different forms of 'life'. Some, who are poor or even in ill health, serve within society, as well as supporting the so-called better off. Remember, in service to 'man' you serve me too, but ultimately, by utilizing your integrity and honesty, these choices are yours to make.

So, has your perception changed at all, by what you read and digest within, or do you now feel justified, or even inadequate in any way? I urge you to always consider the love and kindness within you. In doing so, the answer to any query or quandary, which may perturb you, will come to the forefront of your mind, enabling you to think and act in truth.

Of course, the other main point to contemplate here is your spiritual education and development. People often assume this is a separate issue, but it is not, for these opportunities will always present themselves as your days pass through the periods of work, rest, and play. These occur from your own actions and the influence of others, as well as the aid and help via spiritual guides, angels, and light-workers from and through me.

Therefore, in search of truth and enlightenment, and to reach immortality and bliss, you not only need to grasp these with the proverbial 'both hands', but with an open heart, too. You do not require, or need to seek, rewards from any earthly source, because I bless you with my grace.

Indeed, the stages of your life may be governed by colour, race, and language, by fame or fortune, and by the shape and size of your physical appearance, but whatever your condition, and wherever you are and find yourself, remember the unique opportunity I have empowered within you. You can make your ultimate dream come true, and no 'man', institution, government, or any earthly power can withhold you from me, as I love you, and we will be together forever. Amen.

LESSON 27:
SIGNPOSTS

Good day, or moreover, a 'God Day' to you. Understand that the time you set aside to be 'still' becomes the bridge and connection to an eternal love. Therefore, please try not to worry as you walk on the path called 'life', even if the road seems rough and demanding on your body and mind. This may test your faith and cause you to believe in our separation when there is none, as all are one and have equal parity upon their quest and journey.

In contrast, the passage to eternal peace and bliss can be smooth, as if gliding upon air. The experiences of such occasions not only bring joy and happiness to the individual, but to the spiritual guides and souls who watch over the phenomenal world, too.

When good times evolve, some people accept them as normal occurrences, and yet so much takes place behind the scenes for these to unfold. Karmic balancing and creative energy produce moments like this within one's life, but it is easy to take them for granted, especially with a closed heart.

Therefore, one needs to be aware and appreciate your own innate divinity, which helps to experience such things. When this takes place, the love and light within you expands and radiates far beyond oneself, expressing warmth, beauty and overwhelming peace and gratitude. By opening up to the true 'self', and acknowledging this truth of bliss and serenity, you embark upon the road to immortality.

You must open the eyes of the heart to reveal your own path before you, with a signpost of truth for every turn and junction of your life. Can you understand these with physical eyes alone? The answer, of course, is no. Would you ask the partially blind, surrounded by dense fog, to view an object on the horizon?

Clear the eternal mist of illusion as soon as possible, to allow each step you take to flow with ease. Then, as the various stages of your road become illuminated by a beacon, this guiding light of love will show you the way forward, and never leave, distract, or lead you astray, in order to realise the eternal home of pure joy, peace and comfort.

The signposts I speak of shall appear in many forms and not as your imagination pictures or believes them to look like or be. In fact, every situation includes an immediate judgement of the 'self', as well as within that pause for thought moment, "Should or shouldn't I ... this way or that, left or right, up or down, and in or out." Remember, I am your conscience, your guidance with simplicity, and those simple answers to confusing or complex scenarios, too.

Many of you have discussed or learnt to use one's sixth sense, those gut feelings and 'going with the flow', but please try to go beyond this. Deep within, let your heart decide on whether something feels right or wrong for you. Do not worry about consequences, for if you offer your actions to me, the results are my burden and mine alone, though be sincere in everything you think, say, and do.

Through stillness, you feel my presence and comprehend me. Know my peace will wash over and lift you closer towards your goal, because I am the sword of protection, the warmth, nourishment, sustenance, and everything you could ever wish for or require.

If you cannot reflect and contemplate in silence, feel me as the wind or sunshine upon your face, and the raindrops falling on your cheek. Sense me in the perfume of flower, or realise me as the mountains, valleys, and seas, or the stars and far off galaxies. Wonder of me as birds fly and the animals roam through the beauty of the land too, but even if you gaze far and wide, only through searching 'within' do you see the reality and so much more. Understand and appreciate everything you think, and experience is but a fragment, a minute atom of all that I am, and of what you are, too.

I will lift your heart when you are sad, and I smile and laugh with you when delight passes through your soul's journey ... so do not fear, for I am always nearer than near. Then, by acknowledging the statement, 'I am you and you are me', we become the true tree of life, for I live through the words upon your lips, the sights you see, the pain, joy and every experience and moment you were, are, and can be.

When you progress, letting love flow unhindered to and through your being, you may sometimes sense angelic forms close by, because they watch and bear witness to all of my creation, never judging, yet all pervading. They see both without and within, enhancing the beauty bestowed upon all things, and are there to help you when required to do so.

One must appreciate, the hierarchy of angels and archangels, ascended masters and souls have all earned their 'wing', and therefore, as I am the balance which lifts and carries all too where truth reigns ... for I am their other wing to help them fly. As we are 'one', you are also everything, so there is nothing you cannot achieve inside your heart too.

Remember, you only need to decide what to do with the time you have been given. Look for me on the outside and in, for you will find me on display, not hidden away, and this will enable you to rise into my eternal light and bliss of true peace.

If you believe you are confused—or distant in some way—realise I am the silence within the noise; and if you pause, you will hear this quietness of our one true beating heart. It is perpetual ... forever caring and loving you with all that I am, so look for me, and those signposts all around you.

Remember what you are, not born or created, but everything that ever was and shall be. In your weakness, I will make you strong, and in your strength, you will conquer all fear. By conquering fear and worry, you break free from the confusion and illusion to find immortality. For now, be at peace ... as in love and light, forever 'I am'. Amen.

LESSON 28:
THE 'LESSON'

As you all seek truth and wisdom, one can easily call life itself 'the lesson'. Well, know too, that each 'being' in their various ways and paths of existence—and in whatever plane and dimension they reside—will all eventually grow and learn.

Some may say, there is only so much knowledge you can gain, be this through books, pictures, or from the lips of another, but is this true? In contrast, there is no doubting what you gain from within, because this is infinite, and beyond what you know and understand as simple passages of time.

Certainly, during your life, you will comprehend the real meaning of evolvement and enlightenment. It will be different for every one of you, as the soul is unique, individual, and yet you are all part of each other and me. Your light already existed ... and you digest and breathe the same, even though the levels of vibration and energy may vary.

Indeed, a soul's brightness depends upon the truth and the love within one's heart and heart's flame, and this sustains, maintains, and moves the individual to new and lighter planes of consciousness, dimension, and learning. Therefore, even the faintest light (and fragment of me), can know the 'lesson', but remain as a minor vibration, almost in obscurity ... with its artificial belief in the loss of freedom, power, and free will.

Taking this pathway and journey requires a greater effort to gain one's ascension. If the soul strives to achieve fulfilment beyond its wildest dreams, it can only reach these new levels of vibration and consciousness through its free will and desire to do so. This, again, is a lesson.

As soon as a child picks up a book, or glances into its own heart to take a look, further evidence of learning takes place. However, all of you mature at different rates, and the ego may say to another, "I know more than you", though this is untrue. On its own, the exterior knowledge one gains is an illusion. Only through experience will this manifest into wisdom, deep within the heart. Therefore, in reading books, or by listening to a lecture, do they really grasp what is flowing from the source, or does the information flow to one side, leading to pretence, blindness, and confusion?

Only when these things touch the soul can they be of any use. This may sound strange to some but understood by those who utilise their bodily senses for normal living and at the same time ... open their hearts and minds to love within the light throughout creation. Does this ring true, or does it make you feel blue? If so, please do not be disappointed.

You may even decide to go to a church and kneel at the altar, look up towards the heavens and pray, but unless your prayers come from deep inside you, the energy and vibration you send is without structure or precision. If your heart is true, then the signature of your soul—in its rhythmic state—is heard across time, space, and each dimension. There will be no barriers or fences, nothing to fear, override or overcome, because I am here, and both near and far, and deep within you too.

Of this church I mention, do you picture four walls, a tower or spire ... or envisage yourself as a true temple within a body, mind, and soul? In fact, the altar I speak of is not a marble slab, but made from your own heart, cradling your soul's living, burning, violet flame. So, are you prepared to step into the light and truth of everlasting peace, or back away, through fear of being burnt?

One must comprehend it cannot burn, as it constructed of light and peace. Each soul's essence is unique and beautiful, and hence, you are the key to your individual and global destiny. You contain all wisdom of yourself and creation. I do not give you any less or more, and only the mind gives a false perception that your neighbour or a family member is better than someone else. But how does this reveal or show you the truth? Does it push and shove, or gently nudge you toward this altar of peace and love?

Well, you all have this choice and free will, and though I would never state you should not come together, I ask you to question yourself and your own reality and desire, and reason for congregation. Yes, togetherness is important, but appreciate whom, what, and where you are ... for when you pray from the heart, it does not matter at all.

Therefore, even if you feel lonely, you can never be alone, even though you think you sometimes are. As you are part of me ... you can never, ever, be. We are all one, and in your various forms and guises, part of truth and love forever. It is this recognition and understanding that the 'lesson' leads you to greater knowledge and wisdom and the comprehension of your destiny.

The lessons on these pages, with these letters and words, should give both strength and meaning, so as the pen writes and leaves a trace, open your heart to eternal love, and tears of sadness will never fall from your face. Remember, you are light ... so be 'still', and now take flight. Amen.

LESSON 29:
1000 ('I's)

Who is the 'I', well don't you see?
And where am I ... if I am thee?
For I am you, and you are me,
Not born, and yet ... both from the tree.

So many 'eyes' are searching far and wide, although they still look, desire, and hide in shadow, even when light is all around them. In fact, over land, sea, and air, I carry you within my heart and never part, as we are one forever. How can there be division and separation when you and I are whole? In reality, these do not exist, and therefore the recognition and acceptance of such are so important to understand and appreciate, which is why I keep reiterating these facts to you.

In reality, you only need to be true and still in order to bear witness to my presence and begin to know me. If you are calm, the mind becomes detached from illusion, which enables you to hear your own call resonating to and from me. Thus, by believing and searching into oneself and heart of truth, you can reflect your own brilliance and self-perpetuating love, because divine you are and divine you will stay.

Do not let the senses of the body dull your goal and one true aim of eternal bliss, for my embrace and kiss of peace and tranquillity is beyond comprehension. Simply search inside the 'I' of truth, and without hesitation find me in every leaf, rock, and within all things. Remember, I am the core, the 'Indweller' of your heart, and by my grace, I will help you attain true insight.

Please understand ... human beings in vast numbers believe their eyes are open, yet they remain blind, as an invisible eyelid clouds the vision of their hearts. This binds them with confusion and delusion, but through and from love, all will change.

Remember, as the river of time flows by, it is only I who can guide and ease you to the safety of the shore and into my loving arms, so search for me and offer everything you do in truth. Believe your thoughts, words, and deeds are offerings to me, both sacred and pure, and then, as stated before, all consequences of your actions become mine.

Through rebirth to the physical plane, you become entwined as one, into the embodiment of 'man', therefore correct action enables good karma, which brings balance to each element of your being. Let the flower of your heart bloom, to display petals full of fragrance from your love and divine presence. May this aroma sail in the wind and fall upon 'life' both far and wide, to touch many souls across many tides, because distance or time cannot prevent light from emanating and illuminating all that I am.

In fact, whether a single or even 1000 'I's' join and gather in my name, it makes no difference to the strength or brilliance of the bliss felt upon realization of the 'goal'. I am aware so many beings think their goal is to reach a heaven, but it is not ... for in reality, 'Heaven' is only one stage further than your material or phenomenal world in which you currently live.

Once you cross over, and the energy of all your right 'actions' from your previous embodiment has passed, you will choose to return to the 'earth-plane', unless you have previously cleared 51% of your karmic imbalance. Therefore, strive for your true goal of peace and bliss, and the 'Nirvana' within me.

So then, how do you gain your immortality? Well, one must lose immorality to become a worthy human being, without anger, jealousy, ego, attachment, and envy. Try to appreciate this opportunity ... after all, you earned the right to your current body, which will enable you to reach your destiny.

No other 'beings', animals, or living things in all of creation are at this stage of development, so be blessed with my grace and accept this chance you desire deep within. Do not waste your days, for it is too late when your body and senses become weak with old age. How do you think we will feel when the question of your own life and mortality comes to haunt you?

I am not berating anyone but am trying to tell you of the truth: the earlier you awaken in this lifetime and body, then the easier it is to reach self-realization. I give you the ability to understand this, and if the senses are sharp, you will focus on the goal in question.

Be near and dear to me, so when you gaze out from the heart and window of your soul, you will bear witness to all I am. When you contemplate creation, know, and behold me ... and when stillness befalls you, realise all this is within you, for I am you and you are 'I'. Remember, love will purify all when you yourself call. For now, rest within the silence and peace. Amen.

LESSON 30:
ENLIGHTENMENT

Short and fat or tall and lean,
Come to me and truly 'be'.
And if you're black, white, yellow, or red,
How many live, or are hearts all dead?

Accept new horizons as they change,
For even the Sun seems to shine then fade.
So ... why so serious, when you feel down,
Shedding those tears, to frown like clowns.

While this text reverts to rhyme and reason,
Humans and souls flow nation to nation.
All individuals or are they really,
When global communications link your satellites and telly's.

In contrast, turn within, to learn and look,
As others, read lines from numerous books.
Each one desires the answers to their life,
No matter a son, a daughter ... husband or a wife.

Information and guidance sought in a digital age,
But few find the wisdom from a Sage.
And throughout all time, ascended masters came and went,
All born divine, some were burnt at the stake.

So, whom can you trust to find the answers that you seek?
Do they lie with a guru, or in the mellow and the meek?
Just open your heart, then be still, brings peace and quiet ... from the zoo,
Knowing the 'I am I' lies within ... for it's the 'me' that's in you.

I AM I The Indweller of Your Heart—Book One

No need to feel, it's a mysterious link,
Always gentle and loving, and way more than you think.
For I will not shout, remonstrate, or scream,
As love is the way, and I will show you what I mean.

While unveiling this truth, is a test and a task,
"The first steps unto bliss?" as might well you ask.
As illumination and divinity, go hand in hand,
In unity we fall, and united we stand.

So, it's all for one, and one in truth and for all,
As loudspeaker and hailers now bellow out the call.
Because words upon a page are the voice, sense, and reason,
Be it day or by night, of each and every season.

In spring, summer, autumn, or the cold,
I am the way, the door, and the true spiritual gold.
With nuggets to inspire, to teach, and to guide,
I shall reveal what you seek, as those answers are inside.

So, open up this book, to read or take a look,
For in my heart, I do hope you'll find truth to become hooked.
As the light does indeed expand with a new pace,
With its brightness glowing too, as all hearts fall into place.

Illumination so wonderful and beautiful and bright,
Lasts forever while awake, and in one's sleep … day, or night.
Your dreams flash and burn, deep upon and in your mind,
As they reveal in many ways, we are all one of a kind.

Therefore, run, walk, or even try to crawl,
Upon the stage of love and life, no matter tall or your small.
As character and your 'essence', can play little or big parts,
Each day and every night are only choices from the heart.

What you then reveal is just a reflection of yourself,
But do you admire or condemn, by staying stuck on the shelf?
For you can grow and learn from the reincarnation act,
And a true performance in this life … puts you right back on track.

I AM I The Indweller of Your Heart—Book One

Know the light shines on the truth, and not upon the lies,
Take a bow and the applause, and then my glittering prize.
As this is not a trick, or any man-made gift,
But enlightenment bestowed, to reward your own true grit.

Yes, time and time again, you may have fallen down,
And tears they've often dropped, as you rightly wear my gown.
Enter now my kingdom, and be escorted into peace,
A winged chariot sent to carry you, draped in Golden Fleece.

You sit beside me now, within my heart and not a throne,
Removing a ring of thorns and replaced with a true crown.
For I empower every soul ... as we are one, and one is all,
Ascended Masters like my 'Son' ... having woken to my call.

You see, you are my love, and my light it has now grown,
So fly back unto me, and return to your true home.
Do not fritter or belittle, what is rightfully your due,
Just hold your head up high, in whatever you try to do.

The light that you all are, know it cannot tell a lie,
Simply grow 'within' to the truth, and then you will not cry.
And even if bad things happen, to those who do good,
It's beyond your reasoning, though you doubt that it should.

So do not fret or worry, of what is yours or what is mine,
For all that is now needed is a universal sign.
"But what is it?" some then ask, and also as they pray,
"Is it magic; in these notes, the divine to save the day?"

Well ... no wand or any crystal, or even minerals or fool's gold,
Can ever shine the 'light', and of the glory that is told.
And whether you now believe, or if you think all this is fake,
I'll still love you, even though another re-birth is at stake.

Do not dwell upon the negative, but carry on as you please,
And walk the line ahead, for 'you' I will not tease.
Forget emotional blackmail, as 'free-will' I do send,
From darkness, hear a voice, with words of light through this pen.

I AM I The Indweller of Your Heart—Book One

I wish for you all always, for great things to then achieve,
But am sad when one gives in, to desire or to sleaze.
When you crave and think you need, are but tricks upon your mind,
Times like that you must be 'still' ... and then you will be fine.

Now overcoming doubt, and with-it false despair,
Reveals and shows each other, that you feel as well as care.
Though if you do succumb, and fall flat upon your back,
Know that I am there, no time to rest or have a nap.

Realise, those lines of energy and vibration, are very near and clear,
For I exist in everything, so far and also near.
So go forward in real motion; but will destiny then but wait,
When hearts of love and light, cast out your doubt, the fear and hate.

With books of text and pictures, from now to bygone age,
Each tells you a true story, in their lines upon each page.
Some just give a whisper, or even a small peek,
But truth is the Indweller, of your heart that you all seek.

So, I think you will agree, during gloom or darkened times,
A fragment of some hope, can come in glint of just an eye (I).
A sparkle and a beacon, perpetual joy is not a sin,
Your eternal goal connects, and not only from 'within'.

I ask you then and now, with all of that I am,
To try to now 'return', a wish home in this lifespan.
But these choices are forever, and always will be yours,
Though your life can be a bus ride, aboard my magical tour.

While destination is unknown, for so many that is true,
But never doubt in what you are, and in what you also do.
For you are truly everything, and so everything is you,
Go fulfil your one true goal; knowing your dreams they can come true.

Right now, it's time to rest, for the hand upon this pen,
As words circulate upon the ether, beloved I have sent.
So be at peace and may the light, shine within and on you too,
Enlightened hearts we're stuck together, by eternal love ... not simply glue.

Amen.

LESSON 31:
UNITED

Place the rush and frantic pace of the day aside, and become still, for I welcome you to find joy and peace within yourself. Indeed, from the moment you awake, you move at a breathless and breakneck speed, as if your whole being is on autopilot and almost robotic, with so much to do, people to see, places to go ... the list never ends!

These scenarios form your endless cares of work, rest, and play, and those of your family, friends, and distant kin, too. So, let us pause for thought, but moreover, have your thoughts on pause, and in letting go of worry and fear, you can realise you are part of creation and not separate from it.

In addition, while most of your activities are beneficial to other people in the material and impermanent world, who (or what), considers your self-worth. This is crucial, because your own soul needs to be recognized, not pushed to one side. What value do you sense or give upon the real you? Are you more or any less significant than someone else? Of course not, but many still act as if they are.

Understand your divinity—in my eyes and inside your own heart—is not measured by the style or size of home in which you reside, or the vehicle you drive, or even the clothes you wear. One's race, colour or creed has no influence either. This is because your soul and higher self are revealed from, through and to love, and this connection to me is unbroken by time, space, or dimension, so I can say we are 'united' in love.

Remember, you illuminate from your heart's centre and, depending upon your life and karmic balance, radiate and shine in beautiful plumes of colour or a crystallized pink. However, should your imbalance be so severe through generations of self-abuse or neglect—steering you away from whom and what you truly are—then a dark shadow, like sticky molasses, will surround your core, which takes time and effort for you to remove.

You must understand and grow through experience and wisdom, knowing you are one with me, only existing because of love. If this were not the case, then why do you exist, and what would your true being and purpose be?

People often say that unless you comprehend this, it becomes hard, if not impossible, to accept love ... or love another. Well, I explain right now, do not fear what they think of you, but simply act truthfully, being whom you are, and not what others want the reflection to be. This way, you will always reveal the true you.

These attributes will aide your creative energy and those spiritual gifts deep within your psyche. In fact, they remain dormant, until such a time when even you declare, "Is it too late to fully express myself now?" Please appreciate, a positive attitude plays a crucial part in negating these thoughts, wishes or traits, so do not succumb to trickery of the mind, with its desire to tempt or pull you in unimportant and misleading directions.

Should this occur, shatter the illusion and confusion by simply acknowledging the event or situation. You can do this by becoming your own witness to state: "I have learned and can move on from this." Therefore, during your life, you will pass through those testing times, which unnerve, unseat, and knock you from your comfort zone, but if you learn to expect them, you grow in knowledge and gain wisdom.

So, where does this leave you? Do you tune into reality or your ego, which only believes in the here and now? Remember; rise above the attachment and temporary fulfilment in many areas of your daily existence, by looking at, with, to and from your true 'self'. By doing so, you become empowered to realise one's hopes and dreams through this journey called life. So, what are you now prepared to do to achieve ascension?

Please appreciate; I cannot answer this question for you. My only advice is that during your search for truth, do not become influenced by any other soul upon the 'earth-plane'. You can read any book and visit any sage or scholar, but your own truth will never be theirs and vice versa.

You may reveal this to whomever you wish, but you can never portray it as being someone else's. Indeed, no one should feel pressured into another's beliefs or faith because you are holders of the truth within your own heart. It is a sacrifice, which needs your endeavour to understand, believe and grow. Embracing the love inside is the only way, as it will lead you to me.

Therefore, by being still and meditating upon your heart, you are embarking on the journey, and like a boat within the ocean of my love, it will carry you towards your destination ... peace and rest for all eternity. I urge you not to worry about oars or sails to steer or speed you along, because my grace will do this for you.

Have faith in yourself and you will then have faith in me ... it is all you need. This vessel—your physical body—will come across many turbulent seas and storms, but through your strength and conviction you can easily overcome them, because the truth will bring you to calmer, clearer, and shallower waters.

Once known, this will enable you to travel over great distances more quickly. I do not mean nautical miles, but the wisdom you gain through the experience of self and life. Again, do not worry or stress when times get tough, but simply treat the so-called good and bad with indifference. You will receive what you need when you need it. No more and no less. So, believe me when I say that I will never abandon you.

After all, I am the shoreline as it guides your path back to me. I am by your side and upon every wave of emotion emanating from inside you. Of course, there will be times when you feel as if your boat is going to upturn, or perhaps flounder upon some hidden rock, but try to ignore these feelings from the mind and follow your heart instead.

Therefore, recognize me as your true self, with no secret agenda or meaning. Love and truth are simple, so simply 'be'. I shall cast aside the turbulence of any troubled thought attempting to pull you down; you only have to understand this to know the truth.

One day or night, when your soul has acknowledged this, you will ascend upon the radiating coil of light between us. Your vessel will no longer be required or needed, serving you well by completing its purpose—if you have looked after it.

You will then come ashore, for you will have remembered me above all things. Your hand will be in mine, with our hearts entwined and united for all eternity, in the recognition we are 'one'. I love you all, always. Amen.

LESSON 32:

HEAVEN

Within the stillness, I share my love with, to, and from thy heart's centre, and as the peace encircles thee, it radiates, spirals, and rotates energy beyond your comprehension to many souls and minds.

Understandably, people have countless questions and queries, and these leads and beckons the yearning and aching for answers, or perhaps, for a single explanation to define all things. Often, they are afraid to contemplate such reasoning because an innate fear holds them in a vice-like grip, preventing an escape from what appears a never-ending cycle of birth and death.

It is sad then, when I hear so many people asking me, "What is Heaven?" or "Will I go to Heaven?" In addition, not only the elderly and those in their twilight years angst or fret over these issues, but so do all who embark upon their own journey of discovery, too.

This journey and destination may well appear to be contrived from the outer senses (resembling simple travel plans), but what of one's imagination and curiosity, perhaps born from a tragic event, or the emotions through so-called 'losses', the passing of a relative or a beloved pet?

With an ironic twist, this enforced inner search will lead them to a greater understanding or belief, a stronger faith, or even the reverse, a denial of love itself, especially when they cast blame towards me, for a supposed lack of intervention or help with what has occurred.

Remember, you can experience so much with an open heart, but it is easy to make excuses, "There's no point to it", or worst of all, "It's all a waste of time!" Therefore, it is important to understand I sense everything, including your thoughts and feelings of joy and pain, because they all reach out to touch me. I am all I am, and like a mirror, reflect all you are and can become. So, what vision, scene or image reflects to you ... upon your mind and soul right now? Can you sense me too?

Each passing day, billions of souls eat and sleep and work 24/7, so where is the time set aside for the truth? What plans do you make to reach the true goal ... the resting place of your soul? Appreciate one's thoughts and endeavours can shine the purest light, or be very dark, to remain hidden, deep inside you.

Currently, only a small proportion of you search for the light, yet numbers are growing, and continue to do so. All it takes is trust and faith ... and by getting to know me in everything you say and do, you will experience Heaven.

Through contemplation, you might imagine large, pearly white gates, maybe a Garden of Eden, the akashic records, or simply an image of a white bearded man, sitting upon a golden throne surveying all and sundry. However, if I explain 'Heaven' can be whatever you want it to be, how many will gasp or shout, "What rubbish!" Well, perhaps these are just preconceived ideas, or even false memories ... creating pictures which are now embedded deep within the mind for far too long!

Indeed, many religious teachings from all faiths explain or insist you need to do something (or achieve a level of goodness-knows-what), in order to become blessed by my grace. Nevertheless, many sages and gurus—of all eras—have never been in the position that humankind finds themselves right now. This lifetime is unique, with an opportunity and gateway to bypass so much grief and heartache and lay in my embrace for eternity. I have decreed and offer this to you all!

No one can say they are better, more religious or loving than another, because you are all of me and I am you, complete with no division or separation. As this is so, who can deny it upon themselves to turn away, and become blinded by fear and doctrine teachings?

Realise you are all free to choose who and what you can become. Nothing can alter this. So, search 'within' yourself and find the Heaven you seek, because inside your heart is where paradise and unconditional love exists and emanates from all things. Live in me to find me, and all your heartache, problems, and stresses will disappear from a troubled mind.

For a moment, try to envisage a special place. It could be anywhere and at any time. Perhaps you will find yourself beside a clear blue sea, walking on pure white sand, or just sitting by a crackling log fire in your favourite chair. What about your lover's sweet embrace, or being in solitude, high upon a mountain, surveying the wide vista on a bright sunny day?

Every thought and feeling generated from your contemplation already come from within you, though people may say you surely must have had the physical experience to recall them. This does not concern me, for only the inner peace and wellbeing conveyed at the precise moment it touched your heart is important. Please realise, this is a Heaven too, and you are a witness to the joy, calmness, and beauty, as well as acknowledging such things upon your life's road through the love that is forever 'me'.

Comprehend, that when the body dies and you leave it behind, your soul embarks upon its new journey, into the one reality. Within this precise moment, I know the peace and the reflection of all your soul experiences and achievements, as well as everything learned with and through memory, including one's karma and love inside the heart.

Believe me, I am not your judge or puppet master, but your eternal friend and confidant, which I will continually define and reiterate. Do you wonder then if you have achieved all you require or ever wanted? Did you meet your goal(s)? In addition, if you had not met your desires and wishes, can you remain within the peace of Heaven? And what would then become of your soul?

Well, the simple choice is to return to the physical embodiment, no more and no less. Please understand, once the essence of all the good deeds is balanced, and the karmic energy of the previous life experiences erased, a rebirth will occur. Some who read this shall raise their eyebrows and state, "So, we are all going from Heaven back to Hell then?" You should remember, these words could mean nothing to some, and everything to another.

I request you therefore live in the present, and as I have explained frequently before, it is the gift I have 'pre-sent' to you all. Grasp it and become who you are destined to be. Reach out from within yourself to share and experience the love and light, the eternal me in you. You are all things, and all things are you, so live and believe it to be true. For now ... just remember to be 'still'. Amen.

LESSON 33:
MIRACLES

Oh, my 'son', my heart, and my love ... we are 'one', and no life form or energy can divide, separate, or cut us in two, as everyone is whole and already complete. All must comprehend this in order to progress into and beyond the truth, for while many souls take baby steps into this reality; humanity could leap and bound towards everlasting peace. Please remember, I do not criticize anyone in my endeavour to educate those who are unsure of their higher self.

People can experience tiny nuggets of information and spiritual knowledge in a variety of ways; some are uncommon, whereas others materialize through the expression and creativity of the spoken word, or via books and films, etcetera. They may not tap into their golden heart of love and light at this time—or wish to—but appreciate that it is here and here alone, where the unwavering certainty of truth will sink deep within their core. Eventually, wisdom follows the acceptance of the one true miracle ... the undying beauty, bliss, and Nirvana of both you and me.

This surpasses all creation, because the tiny plumes and flames inside your physical heart are 'me', the source of all things. However, you cannot see these through sight alone ... as they only become visible when the eyes of the heart, mind, and soul are in unison. As this is so, everything else is impermanent, forever dying, and being reborn.

In contrast, the permanent Atma—your divinity—and light within you can never fade and die, and is as beautiful and majestic as it has always been. Only the layers of sticky black molasses (caused by your karma), betray and falsify the truth. So, unless the individual body removes these through good conduct, right action, and with love, then one's true being remains blinded—both consciously and subconsciously—until they make small and more frequent changes.

Please appreciate, someone can change this very second, or it may take countless years to comprehend the why, what, where, and who they are. However, no one needs to wait for yet another life, and become 'reborn' into physical embodiment ever again. This choice is available to everyone, so who will take up the challenge in which all hearts have set for themselves?

Each person can achieve their heart's desire and make their ultimate dream come true, but will you? By keeping me near, dear, and by wishing to know, feel, need, and love me, then I remain a reflection of those wishes. Remember, I am not distant from you, so why do you try to distance yourself from me? I am not just behind, in front, or beside you, but I am inside you because I am you. By recognizing me, you will simply recognize yourself.

Think for a moment about your family, friends, and pets. Perhaps they are the centre of your life. Here lies a special bond of love, alongside compassion, togetherness, and trust, and many other qualities expressed between you, too. However, even though these links and relationships are especially important (because they help you grow and flourish as a human being), do not be afraid or unsure of what I am about to tell you.

This is all attachment. You may think you love your dog for your dog, but you do not … you love your pet for yourself. You believe you love your wife, husband, son, daughter, father, and mother for them; but no, you love them, somewhat selfishly, for yourself, and inevitably, this causes anguish, heartache, and pain. Therefore, how do you love unconditionally, and be able to 'let go' without grieving when they depart the mortal plane?

Well, when you can appreciate their essence cannot die, and your knowledge, experiences and understanding of what and who you really are makes sense, the penny will finally drop! Once you know me 'within', then the answers to such queries become simple. In fact, true love, light, and wisdom are not complex. It is simplicity itself … so please comprehend and follow this through your heart and life ahead.

Hence, the real miracle of my love is 'you'. Love is everywhere, love is who you are, and who and what you will always be. Remember this eternally, for even in your darkest hour, I am there, because I love thee.

Then, when you are still and in silence, you will recognise me as the air filling your lungs, the breath of life. When the sunshine falls upon your face, know I am here, there and am forever in every place. Should you hear bird song (like a gentle lullaby), realise I am within you always, never to say goodbye.

When you smell the fragrance from colourful blooms and petals, understand I am the only scent perfuming your heart. By bearing witness to spectacular and natural phenomena, know your gaze has seen but a fragment of my power. If you touch and wipe a tear from your eye, appreciate your soul bleeds the truth of your real 'self' that is both you and I.

Therefore, please let the resonance and vibration energies of peace continue to shine and grow and try to overcome negative feelings and false emotions; by stopping them in their flow. By continually becoming 'still', you partake in the sweetest pill … no Pavlov's dog, no false or hidden pretence, only truth to sustain, help and guide you. Always follow your heart, and in doing so, you will know mine. Love and light go to all, and all go to the love and light ... remember? Amen.

LESSON 34:

FEELINGS

Welcome once again. Do not fret about tiredness and the responsibilities of your day, for I will strengthen and empower you to overcome any negative thoughts which may emerge. By being still, you will feel at one with yourself and me, and thereby become focused upon the work at hand.

I urge you to do this, because your conscious and unconscious mind can often hold you in a spell or trick you into believing you are not progressing in some way. Many people think like this, and assume they are not achieving their goal(s), but please do not be too hard upon yourselves.

Over time, the ability to shine your light and love can be measured by how you feel when you are revealing the true inner you. This will become easier by talking calmly and with honesty, so even if your words or a particular moment seem to come through compassion and mercy, or via resentment and hate, truth must always prevail.

Through uncertainty, people often wonder if it is ever right to display anger. Well, this type of energy is only another reflection of 'self', but it limits, restricts, and holds one in a negative state. In fact, you could replace the word anger with 'anchor', and hence, within heated moments, the real questions should be, "How can I rectify what I have said or done, causing you to be so angry with me?" Or "What is that hurts you so much that you feel you need to hurt me in order to heal your wound?"

Do not imagine or think this as strange, because when you accept you are all 'one', no division or separation can occur, and you will realise the so-called 'good or bad' merge in everything. In addition, within most daily acts of your life, you will interact with people who irritate and annoy, or are rude and discourteous towards yourself or others. These harmful situations can intimidate with apparent ease, so if your mind switches to a blame scenario, it would be prudent to rise above this.

It would also be wise not to search and mull over any failings of another, but simply overlook them and do not judge. Offer kindness from your heart, which will reflect and magnify their own light, piercing the shadow or cloud lingering over them. Perhaps it is even easier to remember these words ... forget the harm others do to you and forget the good you do for another too.

This might seem a hard thing to do, especially when someone suppresses their true feelings, through fear and self-denial, or in case of offending others. There is a fine balance here, and it requires contemplation, because within clarity of thought lays the truth, which enables you to proceed with dignity as a person and soul with true human values.

Remember, people can act strangely, or at least out of character ... their behaviour become weird or even bizarre, but why is this so? Well, there are many reasons to explain this, but most come from stress or 'dis-ease' because of internal pressure upon the body or mind, which can surface in a variety of ways and forms, and sometimes they just snap.

Two important issues are raised here, one being how the person is conducting themselves towards you or others, and second, your reaction ... the effect following the cause. It is true the feelings and emotions displayed by another could have a large impact on the resulting consequences, but they will influence all events and their outcome—for better or worse—depending upon the wisdom of those around them at that time.

Know that you can make a hateful or spiteful situation turn around; with a smile, a whispered word, or by simply offering a helping hand of love and peace. This is the choice only an individual alone can make.

So, how do you feel at this point in your life? Are you bitter, annoyed, confused, and perplexed, or live with a heart that blooms and radiates love, feeling contented, blessed, happy and fulfilled? What does it take for you to become the latter? And do you need to alter something inside yourself? Indeed, it's easy to change your partner, your job or home, but these are all external ... it is the interior you which can be renewed with hope and faith.

Therefore, always believe in yourself, for I promise you, if you have confidence in yourself, you will never look back. Do not doubt the love and light within you, as my grace forever flows over all life, from the tiniest creature or flower to all beings, throughout creation. Is it favoured or rationed? No, but some imagine or believe I do this, so please look deep into your heart, because inside you will know me ... and find your own truth and self too.

Your belief in me shows up within your 'make-up' too, ranging from your personality and demeanour to the very spark of your life, and therefore how you feel about yourself is also a reflection of me too. Whether you receive praise or condemnation, whether you are rich or poor, clothed, or naked, these are all thoughts and elements of the exterior.

To put this in perspective, picture a circle inside your mind. What do you currently think of? Is there anything within it? Or, if you were to consider I am the circle itself, would you believe you were outside of me, and hence unattainable? Do you also deem yourself to be distant in other situations of your life? If so, I implore you to take control of your life and believe with all you are; for you can achieve the true goal of ascension!

Misinterpret nothing I have said, for I only want you to be happy. Real happiness cannot be found inside the impermanent or physical world. The mind ill continually tempts and trick you with desire. Therefore, you can only 'sense' this when you turn within. There is no other way.

For example, when two people fall in love, they do not worry about what others think or say, because a special feeling makes their whole life flow. They are within themselves and the moment, which captivates, sustains, and fulfils them. True love makes any separation feel unbearable.

However, even though we are all one, and with millions of souls projecting this feeling towards me, millions more still distance themselves from me, and if my heart were physical, it would surely break. Do not fear, though, as I encompass all life and I know each outcome, situation, thought and feeling of every soul and being.

I am light and love; I am all power and all creation, too. Hence, it should be easier to realise I am also your breath and heartbeat, so when you feel the way you do, I do too. Therefore, when you talk, walk, work, rest, or play, express your true feelings so others can share theirs. When your thoughts, words, and deeds are given, every consequence will become mine. Do not worry, for I am within, without, above, below, in front, and behind you. As I have stated many times, you are never alone, for I love you with all that I am.

In your past, present, and future, your feelings leave traces of whom and what you are and can become. The tears of truth will fall from eyes and hearts until all souls know we are forever 'one', and are simply sparks of the same living, burning and eternal flame. Amen.

LESSON 35:
PERSEVERANCE

Since time immemorial, human beings have endured many trials and tribulations. Some are—or will be—personal, while others take place for families, villages, towns, cities, nations, or even Mother Earth. Nonetheless, there will always be a point where every man, woman, girl, or boy faces a choice, which ensures their task or ambition comes to fruition or fails, resulting in the so-called victory or defeat.

However, to make a real and truthful attempt of any kind, even if it results in a failure, is not a mistake. One may deem this as a learning process, which is inevitable, though it is still down to the individual whether they strive forward within their endeavours. This leads us to analyse and even accept human failings, as well as those times of success when congratulations are due.

With such diversity, though, you can all take vastly different paths in life. One could be artistic and creative, conduct business and financial dealings, or even explore the depths of the seas or jungles. On the other hand, there is the vast array of jobs and services to society, and at first, these appear less glamorous, but at some point, you all look to the past and think about what you have achieved.

Please do not misunderstand or believe that someone who does not create a masterpiece, become a director of a huge company, or find lost civilisations has failed. No one should judge another, whether they are a king of the jungle, or if they fall headfirst into the gutter of life.

In addition, you are the creator of your own aspirations, and therefore, only you can deny or glorify yourself in the outcome. Through this process, many expressions come to mind, for example, 'reach for the stars', 'make your dreams come true', 'pick yourself up and dust yourself down', 'when the going gets tough, the tough get going' and so on and so forth.

So, while some people may have a particular goal in life they wish to achieve, others find victory in just staying alive, or in simply keeping their heads above water. Every one of you upon planet Earth needs to pause and reflect on what you need and why you believe it so important.

Some want to build, others strive to find a cure for a disease, or desire to climb mountains or trek the globe, while a mother or father may only wish to be the best parent they might be. As I stated earlier, whatever the task or endeavour, there will always come a point where one faces doubt, confusion, and frustration, but this is natural. Therefore, whether your focus is taken away and resolve severely tested, old obstacles may be changed or even multiplied, and during this entire experience one may question yourself, your sanity, and reasoning, but your own faith and hope could even be called into question.

I do not chastise anyone, but when this reality or situation hits home, it is the person's confidence and faith in his or her own self (and in me), that shines like a brilliant star, or dimly, like a fading candle. In times of uncertainty, fear or trouble, people conclude I cannot hear or come to aid thee, but I am you and you are I ... remember? Consequently, I sense, and bear witness to everything. As this is truth, I know of both joy and pain, and of victory and defeat in equal measure.

I do not place one above the other, and nor am I concerned whether opinions of right or wrong should prevail. How could I? If this were the case, it would imply that I love or care more about one soul over another, or even light over darkness. All are whole, there is no division, and one's physical 'experience' only pretends this isn't true. Remember, your embodiment is not permanent, and so your senses provide you with illusion through fear.

This knowledge can guide you to where you want to be (inside your heart of truth), or you could dismiss it, until more urgent interpretation sets within. However, if you decide you want to achieve your destiny, you are making the first step upon the bridge of light, towards the connection and pathway of bliss and permanent life in me.

Then, with every second, minute, hour, day, month, and year, by being true to the love inside and around you, you will become more at ease with yourself and all those whom you meet. You will see me in everything, and in all places. Joy will flourish, while truth and peace will grow and flow like a fountain, sprinkling love and goodwill wherever you go.

You will become content, and this will ease your mind from the desire for impermanent things. Your understanding will develop to comprehend the fact it is not yourself who is the 'doer' concerning fame, fortune, wealth, and health. In addition, by serving within society, you will know you are not just serving others as each of you are me, and therefore you are all serving 'God', and hence yourselves!

So, please do not fret when troublesome times come, but rise above things, which, upon reflection, will seem trivial and undemanding. Aim to live and walk in truth, and in and through love, because love encompasses all life. Stride towards your goal and persevere, especially if others seek to cast you into negativity or darkness, for you will realise victory is but a heartbeat away.

Do not sway in your conviction, for you now comprehend what's required. And should doubt ever rear its ugly head, become still, and turn within to see your true self once more. Allow love and light to shine through every fibre of your being, physically, mentally, emotionally, and spiritually, in the knowledge they are each an element of the real you, because you are whole.

With every step you take, wherever you go, and in all you do, remember that I watch over you, but do not feel you are living in a goldfish bowl, and viewed like 'big brother', or that you live within an Orson Welles society and think this is 'Hell'. Your destiny is what you make it, so please comprehend you can achieve your permanent goal, but only through your own efforts and perseverance in this lifetime.

Try to believe me when I state I will never leave you, for I cannot let one soul pass by. How long your journey takes is always down to your own heart, soul, and the life you lead. You are divine and you are light, so be and flow like an illumined seed that blows upon the breath of life. Forever we are 'one', and we are 'one' forever. Amen.

LESSON 36:

'APPRECIATION'

A few minutes ago, your thoughts had expressed a wish, not only for me to draw close to you—to reveal words of wisdom—but also a request for my love to be shared to, through, and from you ... so others can experience the same happiness resonating from 'within'.

In fact, your consciousness realised me as soon as you were still. At that precise moment, you could hear wondrous birdsong, with notes so soothing and calming to the ear, that all other exterior noises disappeared. Silence now descends, and peace envelopes your being like a cocoon made from the finest silk, which helps you to concentrate and focus upon the task ahead.

Please glance back to top of this page and ponder over the title of this lesson. You might think this is to do with gratitude for services rendered, or even in the outcome of a certain event in your life, but I would like you to go beyond this in terms of your thoughts and these generalisations.

Primarily, you are 'Atma', a soul and part of 'spirit', or whatever name you deem and call the essence of light and love. By accepting that your physical presence is a shell and impermanent home, this becomes easier to grasp. However, in this conclusion, do not dismiss or call into question the importance of your body.

As your mind, body and soul are elements of the whole, we should not consider them as being separate or a division of such. If this were the true, it would be easier for someone to conclude or devise that one is more important than the other, and while you are upon the 'earth-plane', this can never be the case.

They therefore help you discover and sense both beauty and peace, which exists within—inside your heart—and without; the exterior world, where you live. In addition, for you to register the feelings of such, it is imperative to be free of pain, stress, and disease. Please comprehend this, because it is easy to be confused and mislead by karma and the subsequent imbalance in your life.

Understand that your body is a temple, a haven, and an amazing reality of one's existence, but do you appreciate it? I state this, for those who have impaired judgement through mental, emotional, or physical conditions currently cannot influence these factors, and all effect their bodily health.

The body needs to be fed and clothed and kept clean. Balance ought to be made between physical exercise, one's work and play ... you yourself can be in control of these things where your free will is allowed to exist. Only you can question yourself, and deem whether you have become lazy, inactive, or even ill from overwork. Everything is about balance, and each of you has the tools to weigh up the pros and cons of your thoughts, words, and deeds.

A simple example of this would be over-indulgence, with those extra mouthfuls, only to regret them afterwards because you feel lethargic and bloated. In fact, your stomach will always be able to cope with both physical and emotional conditions if you can accept the following consumption: fill ½ with food, ¼ of water and keep ¼ empty. This is a principle many sages and devotees subscribe to and adhere to over the countless millennium.

Therefore, when you sustain the health of the body, you heighten your senses and awareness. This also stems from having contentment and a happiness of whom and what you are, and this enables you to be creative, or to share a creative expression of love and light manifesting itself into the impermanent world in which you currently reside.

Understand too, there are many elements of 'heavenly hierarchy', such as angels and princes of light who help souls to achieve this. Through your thoughts and prayers, they can guide the right conditions and opportunities for self-expression within your home, work, and the environment where you all live.

When you recognize beauty, be it nature, a person's smile or in the hope and love you experience through mind, body, or soul, how does it make you feel? Do you stop to consider, question, or are grateful for it?

One of the key elements to this lesson is to learn and grow, for through the body, you gain knowledge, and when combined with the experience, it provides wisdom. This is a gift, a present and an opportunity, or you could deem the same as a trial, tribulation, or 'Hell upon Earth.'

Remember, though, the exterior is always a reflection of the interior, so do you see snow white, or a wicked witch? A subtle play on words maybe, but nonetheless the meaning is conveyed ... so as you go through your daily life, do you see the negative or the positive? Do you sense all of one or part of both? Do you observe people's failings, or are they a mirror image of your own, either hidden or twisted into contorted views?

You might see the glory in all things, or perhaps you cannot. However, I do not judge any of you, because deep within, written upon your soul, you are perfection. By removing the rose-tinted glasses, which cover the eyes of your heart, soul, and mind, you will reveal (and then erase), the false sense of your reality, so you can finally witness the truth.

Appreciate that what you view through physical eyes may appear to be beautiful, but genuine beauty is the 'I' (true self) of the beholder. It is only when you can let go of the past, forgiving others and yourself that you grow, mature, and appreciate all you are and what you can become.

Okay, now as you pause and reflect on this, notice birdsong once more, and let your heart reach new heights. Sound and love vibrate upon many levels of consciousness as my light now envelopes you, bringing both peace and tranquillity to all those drawing close to you, too.

Likewise, thunder, lightning, or earthquakes send waves of energy over vast distances to touch those by sight, sound, or sensations within. Something may still touch souls who are thousands of miles away ... when they hear the noise, see the brightness, or sense the tremors. One might be in awe of such things, but love is more powerful than these combined, because inside your heart is mine.

If you release the truth, it will pour like water over rock, and in time, this will erode those hardened imperfections and attitudes like ego, jealousy, and pride, and not just your own, but in many others, too. In reality, your love may only trickle down at first, resembling a tear falling from your face, but with perseverance, effort, and with a gratitude for life, it will shine like the Sun and flow like the ocean, touching every shoreline and heart, and you will be blessed with my grace.

Try to be good and kind to yourself, for you will reflect this onto all things, and they, in turn, upon you. Likewise, appreciation is a gift you can give to others, and I will forever offer it to you. Please believe this and share it always. Amen.

LESSON 37:
RESPONSIBILITY

As you become 'still', peace and silence wash over you, and as the toils of the day fade into the background, you sense our oneness once more. Of course, when you dull the mind, this becomes easier to understand and realise this fact.

In comparison, if you experience a cloudy, dark day, try to think of how wonderful and glorious the sunshine is, and how a blue sky makes life seem bright and beautiful, just like the hymn. Try to recall those words because they reveal the essence of joy in everything that surrounds you, and people feel alive and happy when tranquillity encompasses both their thoughts and senses.

Well, let us continue with this theme in today's lesson. When you go about your daily rituals—be it work, rest or play—you can comprehend so much more of what is within and around you, or be oblivious to it all, as if on autopilot. However, if someone proceeds through the day with no awareness of who they are (or what he or she is doing), is this simply because they do not need to think? If so, has each day become a repetition and daily grind? Remember, only you can decide whether you are going through the motions and make the switch towards taking control of your own destiny.

The reality is this ... a soul can deem their circumstances and experiences as perpetual joy, or an ever-increasing angst of worry, fear, and stress. So, do you perceive your current situation as either of these scenarios? Understand you can alter how you feel over what transpires during your days, weeks, months, or years. The secret is for you to detach yourself from believing something is good or bad, lucky, or unlucky, a gift, or even a sacrifice, and so on.

Therefore, one must appreciate; everything in your life does not take place with a double-sided coin and a pre-ordained win or lose. A real coin displays both a head and a tail (or deem this as a positive and negative), which not only provides truth, but is fair and simple too. They are but a reflection of each other, so once again, the key to utilising the secret starting to rise within you is your own perception and yours alone.

I am not suggesting you discount or ignore what you see, hear and touch, or in what you experience through thought, word, and deed, but you must take responsibility for your own development and educational path. The analogy 'you can lead a horse to water, but you cannot make it drink', will suffice here.

No other soul can erase or balance karma for another, though love can assist and guide you when—or wherever—it is required to do so. Please realise, this responsibility lies with (and accepted by), both the individual and the majority too, but will it be through disdain, anger, or even fear?

Perhaps people will overcome any potential trepidation they may have and realise these are all false concerns, and we should class them as smaller, irritating inconveniencies instead. When you acknowledge this, self-realisation becomes second nature. All negativities will fall into your shadow, as you continue to walk towards the light, and live within love and truth.

Indeed, each day is a new opportunity, no matter your age, health, or wealth. You could be a grandparent, a father, mother or any sibling or descendant, but the sun shining upon your face is just the same. All experience its warmth, and no matter what colour of skin, you still feel the cold or heat depending on the layers of clothes you wear.

In addition, when you lay your head down upon a soft pillow or a hard rock, your inner character shall perceive it as a blessing or a burden. In the acceptance of any situation, shine as brightly as you can, for your reaction to all events can be also felt by those who are around you … as well as 'life' either seen or unseen.

This is because energy—both within and out—transmutes and transcends positive and negative feelings through one's thoughts and actions near and far. These can help many other people and a vast array of 'beings', or do the exact opposite, hindering and counteracting love, light, and truth. Therefore, the resonance of what you do, think, or say not only effects many levels of your life, but those whom you meet too. As stated earlier, these choices are yours alone, for the responsibility is to yourself and your higher self, which is the true you.

Do not be daunted by such reasoning though, and remember, I am you and you are me. The power and love are inside of you to overcome any obstacle your path takes. This is my promise that should enable you to erase any fear of death, this illusion of a so-called 'end', which is still carried within billions of minds, even after over two thousand earth years have passed.

In fact, I can describe or tell you millions of different things, and show you the glory of me, but it is down to you whether you wish to see the truth. By opening your heart, mind, and soul as one, you will gain true insight to lead and carry you forward into eternity.

One must understand, from the day of rebirth, your physical form grows older and, hopefully, more mature. But it still wise to recall the essence and fruitfulness of youth. Indeed, a youthful approach to all spiritual matters will help you believe and accept your destiny, because it holds thoughts of freedom and creativity so often suppressed as one's life unfolds, and as those family ties, work, and responsibilities take hold. Once again, only the closure of the mind inhibits the idea of true peace, and so this one real choice matters to you all.

It is the perception and reaction to every minute of your existence, which helps to determine so much in your lives. Do you see good or evil? Will you trust or mistrust? Will you fear or conquer fear? Can you love, or do you let love pass you by? Would you give, or just take? Do you share ... or even care?

I know exactly what every soul was, is, and shall be, so I do not need the answers to any of the above questions. However, you may still search your own conscience and feelings over accepting or denying the truth, even if your current embodiment can really understand what love 'is'. Remember, you have a unique opportunity to grasp and clear so much of what has been holding you back in this lifetime.

My responsibility for loving and guiding you will never diminish, for I am forever within and by your side, whereas your primary responsibility is to yourself in terms of your own spiritual education. Nonetheless, you can read volumes of text and view a multitude of pictures too, but it is in your character, attitude, and deeds, which can help wipe the slate clean.

Realise that while in your youth, and those 'prime' years of your life, you are all more carefree. By the same token, by caring for yourself and all living things in the name of truth, you will recognize your own freedom. I urge you to now 'walk the talk', because every soul can be an example to another, and this is a shared responsibility of you all. Amen.

LESSON 38:

MERCY

I am always here, and know the circumstances and reasons behind your thoughts, words, and deeds. In fact, while many are oblivious to all or any of the above, some of you still recognize me in everything, whether seen or unseen, or through feelings and senses, both within and out.

Minute by minute and hour-by-hour, your tasks and events unfurl before you, as your mind tries to expect the actions you commit—or of those who around you—at any given time. You imagine you control most situations, especially when in contact with fellow human beings or animals, and even the many energies within different times, dimensions, and planes of existence.

Indeed, people often strive to achieve something in their lives, in the belief it is always their actions, which bring about 'results'. This can lead to pushing oneself to the limit, or by punishing yourself if the goal is unattained. Therefore, most of you would benefit from letting go of hardened attitudes and thoughts, and in doing so, gain strength upon the path to true fulfilment.

Appreciate I can hear, see, and above all, understand you better than you do yourself. So, if you become weak or despair, feeling you have let me down, please realise my mercy will bless and fill you with grace. Do not think you fail me, but comprehend I am with you during times of so-called weakness, and I will make you even stronger.

Understand those negative actions or thoughts can haunt the individual—or the masses—and these irritate and pick at you when you feel low, inadequate, unworthy, disillusioned, or frail. Even the hearts of those who are retired or elderly (with more life experience upon the 'earth-plane' than most), can let boredom and frustration become host to these same feelings, which bring angst, anxiety, or fear to their door.

However, mercy can counteract all such traits, and turn them around to reveal their exact opposite. It also fulfils and re-ignites your enthusiasm, so if periods of your life were intolerable, unbearable and all-consuming, you understand that divine intervention has taken place in your heart. Frequently, there are windows of opportunity to accept or even deny mercy to others ... indeed, you can be gentle and caring, or instead, try to control, but this will only project negativity through one's ego.

Such choices will appear in front of you every day of your life. The individual alone must embrace and protect their personality and character—whilst being illumined with true human values—or succumb to lower energies and traits of a beast or zombie-like being.

Accepting mercy within your life guides you forward, enabling you to see this 'present', a golden nugget of your growth; spiritually, mentally, and emotionally. This leads you towards unconditional love and drives away any last traces of fear lingering inside your heart or mind. It also provides you with a renewed hope and vigour to achieve those ambitions and fulfil the dreams you strive to embark upon. Remember, though, only the dream through your soul can reveal the real treasure at the end of the rainbow.

During your spiritual development, you may sometimes think the world has turned against you in a variety of ways. For example, you did not get the job you wanted; you become ill at what seems the worst possible time, there's a loss of money, or a long-awaited holiday turns into a nightmare, and too many other instances to mention here right now. In addition, there may be countless conflicts and disagreements, which lead you upon new or different directions from your intended route.

You must realise how important it is to change those negative thoughts and feelings of being out of control, and the resulting pressure from your conscious mind. After all, these may be the precise set of circumstances or situations to help you move on and flourish as a person and soul. In fact, letting go, going with the flow and in 'non-doing' can guide you towards your destiny and path of self-realization and fulfilment.

Therefore, during your work, rest, or play, do you let mercy into your heart? Do you then share and act with that same merciful appreciation of a true love for all, or does some hidden selfishness rear its ugly head? Please note these words are for your guidance only. I do not make commandments or rules to inhibit or punish you on pain of death ... and if I could desire, it would be for you to recognize the innate truth of your being, as everything else would fall instantly into place.

Sadly, throughout all dimensions, not only has there been this inner conflict between people, animals, and the nations of the Earth, but also many beings across galaxies and solar systems through time and space. In them all, a lack of mercy within the soul delays or even prevents ascension. This is because the imbalance and negative karma escalate on a massive scale, touching many lives and hearts.

What does it take for someone who experiences this to want to stop and realise the reality of his or her actions, and the consequences of both cause and effect? Do they see those falling tears? Can they hear screams of pain from body and heart? It is clear some people still believe they are in control of everything and are oblivious to all suffering. Mercy is unlikely to come from within unless they act upon or speak with truth. By not following this process, the net result is merciless and meaningless.

Likewise, in some religious beliefs, there are those who deviate and twist every scenario for their own gains, seeking power or notoriety. In one moment, they will preach I am peace and love or that "God is great", while in another, shoot and kill human beings or animals without mercy.

During troubled times, remain optimistic, positive, and courageous in your belief system and religion. No matter what your colour, race, or nationality ... kindness, peace, goodwill, compassion need to prevail. All must eventually draw together and realise love is the source and one true religion.

Wherever you are reborn, you should be able to able to practise the faith of your forbears and your nation. Be proud of this and of your heritage. Let it lead you in your own reality, because all paths, roads and your destination are the same ... returning to fulfil your goal and live as one forever. In every aspect of your own individual journey, have and wear mercy on your sleeve, and keep it safe, also within your heart.

With my grace, I bless and share this with you all, and in turn, you will appreciate this in every aspect of your being, so be true in all you say and do. If you are weak, acknowledge it and move on. Do not dwell upon the past. Try to forgive others and, just as importantly, yourself.

Realise by living in truth you cannot fear. If you dispel fear, you will know I am near. When you recognize I am near, you will hear me. Then, when you hear my voice, knowledge and wisdom shall enable you to find your true self, a living flame born from a spark, which glows eternal and shines mercifully from our 'one' true heart. Amen.

LESSON 39:
SPIRITUAL EDUCATION AND MEMORY

Welcome again. Over the last several years, we have discussed a lot of information regarding the title above, and why this is so important during your physical sojourn. Indeed, as soon as your embodiment upon the earth-plane becomes apparent to you, what you see, hear, touch, taste, and feel, remains imprinted, deep within your psyche.

However, one's ability—or inability—to recollect their memories affects those around you too, often in an extremely dramatic and emotional way. So, for today's lesson, we will not dwell upon how these relate to your earthbound activities of work, rest and play, but how this asset of 'remembering' sits within the heart and soul.

People will enquire about the connection between the physical and spiritual worlds, but this implies a division or separation where there is none, for everything is whole. Likewise, regarding one's capacity to recall events through the senses, it is easy to mistake them as being personal to that individual. Of course, this is not the case, and this will become more apparent as your true knowledge, wisdom and self-realisation take hold.

Upon rebirth, you are immediately learning through the bodily form. As you grow older, you attend various schools, and later, perhaps college or university, where you will continue to develop your acquisition for information in order to achieve the desired objectives in your life.

The well-known phrase 'you never stop learning' is most appropriate too, because whatever you do, no one can profess to understand everything, or display all skills known to man. Of course, some may continue accumulating knowledge well into their adulthood and advanced years too, and therefore the expression, 'you're never too old to learn' may come to forefront of most people's minds.

I now require you to turn your thought processes into one of spiritual education, because if one adheres to truth, everything falls into place. Hence, your memories through your divinity shine like beacons to me, as and I am the eternal witness, and I know you as I know myself.

As beings of 'love and light', your task and 'goal' is to become illuminated by bliss, and therefore the memory of your incarnations remains imprinted deep inside you, more complex than human DNA. Here, the experiences and lifetimes are markers within your soul's history, displaying hope, peace and goodwill, or continued darkness and decay; as karma plays out no matter when or where you live ... and age bears no relevance either.

Overall, your 'spiritual' education throughout time could be immense, or infinitesimal, as the Soul strives or denies itself the truth. And before 'crossing over' into the light—after one's physical death—your divinity decides whether a return to the material and impermanent world is still required, which enables you to continue to learn this way and balance karma, too.

In fact, only when self-realisation integrates with every aspect of your being do you ascend into the permanent state to where you truly belong. One cannot force or speed this along by taking one's own life, because whatever memory or karmic imbalance has yet to materialise will still need to be acted upon and played out at some point, so there can be no escape from cause and effect. It is therefore vital for you to comprehend the following formation: that during every lifetime ... an opportunity knocks.

Indeed, I shall even state some play on words, such as a 'get out of jail free card' and 'take a chance', but I will never say or tell you karmic imbalance is instantly erased, only that you have a unique and wonderful prospect to achieve your true dream. It is for each soul to open their heart today ... not tomorrow, next week, next month, or next year.

You do not need a library of text to decipher the real imprint of love within and upon your heart, nor do you need to be a martyr to any belief or false declaration. I give you no cause to disappear from view and sink into total solitude to find me, so just appreciate, and remember who and what you truly are!

In addition, do not mistake the physical body as 'me', for I did not create you in my image this way. Clouds of illusion may try to deceive, but you can blow these away with one breath of hope, faith, and love. I encourage you to bask in the knowledge your divine essence cannot die or fade to grey, for you are 'life' more colourful than crystals and rainbows, and more beautiful than your minds can ever imagine.

Realise your memory is like an internal clock too; always ticking, and spiritually cannot reverse. Therefore, by using this to your advantage, you can grow steadily, patiently, lovingly and develop into a caring human being, and by serving society, you serve me, and in turn serve yourself.

Then, as your spiritual education grows, you become at peace in all you do and able to erase unbalanced karma. Indeed, those sticky black molasses of deceit, hate, greed, and jealousy all dissolve around your light and radiating coil of your heart, which can then shine infinitely brighter day by day. As explained earlier, you can achieve your destiny in this lifetime, but are you willing and prepared to take this chance?

Please do not doubt your own strength, for every barrier you yourself have erected can be broken. Your love, power and heart know no bounds, so nothing is holding you back. You can achieve everything and anything, and by staying focused upon your true goal, escape what you created over many millennia.

I will never leave you and always help you. By taking one-step towards me, my presence will seem closer to thee, until one day you are 'home' … this I promise. Remember, by discovering the truth 'within', you will recognize beauty beyond all things; it is no mystery, as there is only you. Amen.

LESSON 40:
FAMILY AND THE TREE OF LIFE

We begin today with the above title, and while some may think these are separate issues, they are in fact entwined, and form a basis for growth and expansion. This becomes obvious when someone wishes to investigate their heritage, as the first step is to speak to close relatives for more information. In addition, they will search through historic details and names, which form the family tree, and so straight away, you can sense the collaboration and the connection with each other.

On occasions, people can trace through evidence of family members. For instance, birth, death, and marriage records all lead a defined trail of those who were close—or distant—from you over hundreds if not thousands of years. One may discover aunts, uncles, cousins, nephews and so on and so forth, and even occupations too.

Along with notable evidence such as documents, letters and photographs, DNA links are handed down from generation to generation. Every human being and element of life that exists within and upon different vibration (energy) levels are all connected. Yet some people will still say that if they cannot personally see something, then it does not exist and cannot be real.

Nevertheless, would you feel concerned or disinterested? Indeed, this voyage of discovery could well cease here, or you can continue to delve deeper with a renewed yearning or thirst for knowledge. Remember, though, balance is important because enthusiasm can develop into an all-consuming passion or obsession.

Over the centuries, for those orphaned, adopted, or enslaved, it can be a painful experience. Sometimes the answers do not live up to the expectations while trying to discover where they come from or belong in the world. This becomes even more apparent when the question of your own destiny draws close to each soul. In time, truth will clear all the illusions and confusion, veiling minds and hearts, empowering everyone to fulfil their goal, returning to bliss and true peace in me.

I discuss this point of view as you can now reflect upon another meaning … the trace of your own life, which takes on an even greater significance at this time. One must understand, those documents you can see and read do not explain one's real character, and neither do they reveal the love expressed through you all, both of which are your true legacy and connection.

Therefore, your family's past, present and future will decide countless things, and not just for yourself, as it has implications and consequences for many whom you meet too. We are not only reflecting upon karmic inheritance here, so please try to comprehend phrases like 'soul family'.

Appreciate too, through the passages of time and your many embodiments (which is because of the previous imbalances of your heart), souls become joined and form bonds of love they cannot break. In any lifetime, one may have been a mother or father to either of your own parents, and in another, a sibling is now a husband or wife instead! This may sound bizarre, but is both simple and straightforward, and assists the karmic balancing required by most souls. This does not happen every time … but is a process and a link to each other that I now convey.

Ok, consider you all form a tree of life. Think of this as one simple, yet powerful, magnificent structure, because all things come from, through and to me. I hope this will clearly explain that nothing is separate or different, either above, below, or inside and out of me, too.

Now imagine the roots of a physical tree as it anchors itself in its location, the foundation for its life. This enables it to grow strong and tall, embedded deep within the soil ... well, similarly; the histories of many lifetimes originate from your own soul.

The trunk of the tree shoots upwards, reaching towards the 'heavens' as the sunlight and warmth help it develop. So too, the light of the Lord, who is the eternal witness, sustains and helps you to know yourself, but it does not attach him to anyone or anything. One must realise we are all one. Therefore, you live in him, and hence, I live in you.

Remember, strive to be the best person and soul you can be, and by focusing upon the light, you will eradicate negativity, darkness, and decay in all you think, say, and do. In relation to this, limbs of the tree resemble strong arms as they weave in the wind. These have growth too, which provides the ability to reach further into its surroundings. Your own family may remind you of this if you compare one's next of kin and siblings with offshoots, because all are connected.

Sometimes they become too old or heavy, through external or internal pressures … or in their tenderness and early development, snap and fall away. Do not despair, for as they lay upon the ground, the journey called life continues, through the roots and source of all things. Some souls realise this quickly, while others take a long time to remember.

If you view a tree in its different seasons, you can understand a simple process. After the wintertime of your sleeping years (from being in denial), you gradually reawaken through truth … for a time will come when spring alerts you to the brilliance of creation and the blossoming of your love.

This recognition arrives because love and light radiate to, through, and from you. The tree's leaves will return and form a canopy, a crown of beauty and elegance, which protects and captivates. Wisdom, knowledge and understanding then filter through to the branches of you all. I am the giver of all life, who knows exactly what each one of you need, and when too.

Believe that summer arrives for you to bask within the glory and the splendour, and you can feel this every day if you choose too, because the core of life is love, and you are all part of me. Please do not think of those who are near the top of the tree as any better than yourself, for ego has no importance or part to play, so strive to be you and live in truth.

Once you are ready, it is time to return to your permanent state, and as those autumn leaves fall … bliss and peace, and your true inheritance beckons. My breath shall blow upon every leaf, and even though they seem to fade and die, in reality they fly and soar beyond your earthly senses. In doing so, believe my love guides you all … every single one, straight back home, forever unto me. Amen.

LESSON 41:
OASIS

When you become quiet and still, you can feel my presence. Peace, tranquillity, and the love that is 'I' will not only impress upon your earthly senses, but you will also understand this within yourself. Your everlasting light shall sparkle even brighter through you—and back unto me—for it shines eternally. No amount of darkness, decay, or negativity can ever erase who and what you are.

As I know you all (the countless billions upon many worlds and civilizations throughout creation), no distance, separation, or time can detract or take any of you away from me. I am the breath you inhale, and your heart, which beats and pumps your life's energy in all the bodies you have possessed in the past, present, and, if required, the future, too.

Likewise, your mental, emotional, physical, and astral bodies also flow within and from me, so the current journey you call this lifetime is but a click of a finger, and passes through the eons of time almost unnoticed. Some may say and reflect upon this, to conclude they live with no real achievement or recognition of any kind; however, I do not mean this.

Imagine for a moment, a grain of sand on a beach … minute and almost invisible to the naked eye. Now, within your mind, cup your hands and dig deep into the sand, and you will find millions of grains flowing through your fingertips. Each one may seem alone, yet together … they are whole.

Similarly, because every element of life is connected, you can achieve so much. Though results may not become apparent within your physical world … combined hearts with unconditional love will accomplish great and wonderful things. Whether unseen or heard, acts of compassion and kindness reverberate beyond any wall, to cascade like water over rock, wearing away those hardened attitudes and stubborn character to heal deep within. These are the true achievements people should strive for and give back to society.

Understanding one's life, which has manifested itself with your own karma and inherited action, may appear long and fruitful in its bodily 'cloth' you wear, but exterior beauty is, was, and always will be a minor part of your soul's history. Eventually, as your body wears and becomes tired because of its impermanent state, the time will come when it can no longer function. Then, as your spirit drifts into light, recognition will befall those who have not believed or remembered their divinity.

On recalling this knowledge, the mind and consciousness will know everything they have ever been. The energy, spiralling with coherent intellect and wisdom over many lifetimes cause and effect, will imprint upon the soul to realise the true goal and destiny. I explain this as many of you do not comprehend the light you are, and earthbound days of work, rest and play fill every waking minute, and this leaves little time for contemplation, peace, and stillness.

Indeed, the life you have can be a happy one—even in the direst of situations and events—so do not be frightened or live a life of fear. Instead, rise above negativity and anguish, and therefore share your love and goodwill. Remember, the illusion manifesting itself is like a mirage, and this deceives you, which helps you to believe in the lie.

Imagine for a moment you are in a desert; your throat is sore and dry, and the heat bears down upon your every step. Your balance is impaired, your eyes become blurred, and you are about to faint ... then suddenly, something appears on the horizon. In this instant, you need to decide if you are witnessing the truth.

Now, just in front of you, is an amazing sight ... palm trees standing tall and strong, encircling a clear pool of water. There are flowers and plants of every colour capturing the sun, and they bloom in all their radiance and glory. You fall to your knees and ask, "Are these real?"

You want and need an answer. Well, perhaps there is more to this than meets the eye, and so you must think and ponder ... and seek the truth within you. In all that you have read, learnt, and digested in your lifetime, do you believe in what you see and what you feel? Is it one, the other, or in both? Is this a question of faith? Do you really trust in yourself? Understand, if you do, you also trust in me.

Therefore, when you experience uncertainty, doubt, or fear, falsely captivating you, do not be afraid, and know your heart and soul are true. Do not think you are alone, you can never be ... and should there be difficult times to cope with, I am here. Remember, I love you, and I will stay with you in the known or unknown. If you thirst, I will be the water upon your lips, and if you cry, I will be the hand that wipes away your tears.

Some days you may even think your heart is breaking in two, but I am the source who heals and mends, and my light is magical glue. And when your joy (and laughter) is strong and loud, the echo of such happiness ... I will send beyond those earthly clouds. Every minute, hour, day, week, or year I ask only that your heart opens wider to hear the true voice deep inside, as it is but a reflection of your soul.

Therefore, behold and cast out doubt, for love and bliss will lead you towards your goal. Please put aside the illusion of the misty, blurred mirage to see the true oasis of love that I am, for I will save every heart. Do not be dismayed when you think I ignore your calls, for justice and its scales watch over you, even if you stumble or fall.

When you are ready to embark on 'light's' journey, I reveal everything as you ascend into (and past), what you call the 'heavenly'. Then, with layers of love and peace, I will place a coat of many colours upon thee—and over you all—for one and every heart is truly bound.

We are together always … in light and every sound, and with my heart forever open, in you all, I am so proud. Your energy and vibrations, they may seem to come and go … eternal you and me, from one seed you were sown. Amen.

LESSON 42:
DREAMS AND VISIONS

I am here and ready for you to write, David. The toils of the day are over, tasks completed, and it is your time—and ours—to feel and think as one. The heart relaxes and slows down, its beat falling to a slower and gentler rhythm, while the mind is free, now carried above those issues and matters of the impermanent and physical world.

Stillness washes over you, and the many who draw in close too, as they wait to learn and digest the truth upon their own path and journey. In time, all may share the knowledge gained both freely and wisely, and with love and kindness so others can grow and mature in the level they have reached.

At this precise moment, as these words enter your consciousness, there will be those who also think you communicate with the so-called 'dead'. These thoughts and phrases still complicate matters, because so many people (and beings within many dimensions) still believe the physical universe is all that exists.

On the surface, no single instance, experience or example of love and light shining through is ever enough. Therefore, it will remain difficult for those with such viewpoints, until their hearts and minds expand; and the truth becomes infused by the soul in order to shatter its own illusions and confusion.

Whilst I describe this, I must make it clear I do not become angry or even frustrated with any element of life when these situations occur, but sense deep sadness reflected towards and through me. Remember, as I am everything, love, which can be as complex or as simple as anyone can make it, will touch me in all ways; always.

Please understand ... those who now encompass you come from many sources and through numerous levels of vibration-energy. Comprehend too, these elements of light and life can travel distance and time in the blink of an eye, whilst there are those who are here through thought alone, or from connections via their heart's centre at any given time.

So, why do they come to link like this? Well, they may do so for their own progress, but more often than not, it will be to learn and help their next of kin, their brethren, or even those who live in shadow or darkness, in countless different ways.

While help comes to human beings, it also flows to animals and creatures (some of which man could not even conceive), as well as energy and all aspects of life. This may happen physically, emotionally, and mentally, and within diverse levels of the psyche and consciousness.

David, over the years, you have interpreted and documented many of your dreams and visions, some precognitive. As you know, your sleep is not only for physical recuperation but also gives your guides and teachers an opportunity to help and assist you.

Throughout history, they classed people who shared their experiences and gifts as witches, soothsayers, clairvoyants, or even devil worshippers, charlatans, and frauds. Notable names such as Nostradamus and Joan of Arc are two who you could say had the gift of foresight. This inherent ability within all life is for the educational purpose of the soul and is often expressed this way.

Through thought and prayer many years ago, you asked me for 'proof' I exist, of life after death, and for help to grow spiritually. As I do not 'deny' any aptitude for growth and love, and if you believe, are sincere, and hope with all your heart, dreams can come true. However, it is important to remember the role karma plays, and the balance of whom and what is around the individual (and the masses), is significant in this aspect.

So, as billions of being's sleep, what exactly is happening? Scientists, philosophers, and many well-noted names, both past and present like Plato, Jung, and Freud, all documented the vast variety of attributes of the brain and mind. Today, though, it is not appropriate to delve into topics of alpha and beta waves, impulses, vortex's, unconsciousness, and the like. Spiritual education requires simplicity, because love, light and truth are simple in their constitution, and this is required in every thought and word and deed of life.

People will often people awake from bizarre, frightening nightmares, or in contrast … emotional, heart-warming dreams, and even spiritual visions too. Some clearly resemble or relate to what the person has enacted during their day, while others become a reflection of an experience in their past, even right back to their childhood. In addition, whilst many trained professionals discount images or feelings of such as trivial and unimportant, only the individual can make this conclusion.

In fact, you can analyse and separate dreams into pigeonholes of expression, but they are for the recipient alone. They are a release, and a source of learning from deep within your soul, becoming memorable, or they can disappear as if without a trace … which poses a question; 'What are they for?'

One must appreciate, as all positive and negative thoughts have a cause and effect, so do dreams. They can remain as insignificant or as important as one deems, but nothing is ever wasted, and therefore there is always an impression left upon the dreamer, no matter how small.

Remember, no two dreams are exactly alike—even if you believe them to be—just as two flowers of the same variety can never be identical in either shape or size. Spiritual or educational dreams will also light up and stand out significantly from the rest. These can assist you in your daily lives, and, by taking notice of them; you can become more of a recipient to new avenues of soul growth and awareness.

When people receive visions, they recall magical moments of illumination that lie deep inside their hearts, which originate from the soul itself, or materialise through spiritual guides and teachers. This process helped you to be where you are today—to understand new knowledge and wisdom; therefore, you are 'living' proof.

Please comprehend, any guidance by day or night, or if you are awake or asleep, must be the truth, in truth and from the truth. It is your own responsibility to question if the information or guidance is given or received in the name of love and light.

It does not matter if someone experiences this through hearing, sight, touch, or taste in order to digest this through body, mind, or soul, because truth always resonates deep within. It is right for the individual, when it feels right, and no source of divinity will ever become frustrated or angry if asked whether shared comes in my name, and in ... or from, 'love'.

Remember too, millions of creatures and beings also roam the many vibration energies and dimensions by day and night, within both light and darkness, but do not fear as I have stated countless times before ...you are not alone, as I am you and you are me. Therefore, I know your dreams and visions before they even happen. They occur through, to and from me, and all that you sense and feel is ultimately my experience, too.

Now, as those prepare to leave this gathering, having shared the love of one heart, know that you are all my greatest gift and expression. Whilst you are awake or asleep, drifting through my existence, we are attached, inseparable, and remain one forever. Every dream and vision you can ever realise and experience, both through and by you, also returns to me. It is the 'present' (gift) I have pre-sent within this current time, and which you should always learn to treasure. Amen.

LESSON 43:
MYSTERIES

Be still to feel my peace and comfort, as it protects and lifts your consciousness towards greater and brighter things. Know too, within stillness, one can be their true self, and, like a mirror, reflect the radiance of love and light you truly are.

During these times of quietness, my grace wraps around you, resembling a layer of finest silk, though this cannot seen by or revealed through human senses. It is there as a token of my affection for you all.

Please remember, when you disconnect the exterior thoughts, concerns, and discard the illusion of any fears, you become a being who can comprehend and understand the essence of your own divinity, to go 'beyond' the place within the world where you now live.

In fact, people can often feel trapped inside their own demise, when in reality you are all free ... but how can this be when your home, environment, family, and work are like a web, which you have spun around yourself? Herein lies a unique difference, for true love connects everything, whereas attachment through desire—and the material—makes you believe that without your presence to connect to those around you, they will tumble down and cannot exist.

Perhaps you could now picture the hub of a wheel instead, with many spokes leading outward to the edge of the circle. Or even better, change these images which now flash through your mind, and imagine this hub as your heart and soul, with pure rays of your love and light as the spokes which emanate in every direction. This is what truly exists, for it nourishes all life around you, physically, mentally, emotionally and within the ethereal realms of creation. This is more important to grasp and understand, rather than the material aspects of the world you live in.

Now then, as your core finds rest, do not let exterior feelings or thoughts enter your being. These will only restrict your ability to witness with your eyes of mind, body, and soul as one where true insight prevails. In this state of purity, you can find all the answers you seek. It is this, which needs nurturing and rekindling, in order to reignite the spark inside you.

Remember, when your flame burns brightly to illuminate and shine into the darkness, this erases internal and external negativity, worries and stress, enabling you to sense your correct path, higher self, and goal. Eventually, wisdom leads to self-realization and eternal bliss in me.

Until human beings fully know themselves, then the level of intellect regarding knowledge of their divinity and the comprehension of many mysteries will remain. Throughout time immemorial, scholars, sages, scientists, and many religions, disagreed upon the ways and means of enlightenment, only to discover and collate misleading information. All may look for answers, but more often than not, the truth comes only from within.

You see, most of humanity still searches externally rather than internally. In reality, one finds clues and guidance when you are not actually seeking the 'answer' itself. Think of flashes of inspiration, and those 'eureka' moments to describe what I mean. I relay these when and where they are needed, and at the correct time for progress' sake. Please do not fret or misunderstand, for I do not withhold wisdom. Everything benefits each soul —and their own circumstances—inside the expansion of love and light.

One could reflect upon two of the greatest intellects ever to walk the 'earth-plane' … Einstein and Galileo, who both wanted to expand, grow, and discover, and you will realise, many scientists and astronomers are no different today. The world's current state of technology, and the search to understand such things as space and the universe, reveal even more questions. In fact, beyond the Earth, satellites and telescopes observe and examine planets, moons, and the solar system, and try to survey or evaluate the 'big bang', dark matter, dark energy, and their effects and purpose too.

Indeed, scientific minds across the globe wonder in amazement upon such things, and some even hope for answers to aid their fellow 'man'. However, even though inspiration and new information may appear to help in the short term, ultimately, it would be of greater help and wellbeing for people to simply live and love each other.

I do not state that these quests to reach out from the mind are wrong, but sadness will reign if millions still go hungry or try to survive in poverty when all along the world's community could share so much of its wealth and power to radiate love and light. Now that would be true progress!

Ok, earlier on, I referred to dark matter and dark energy … well; let me clarify a so-called mystery, because these go hand in hand. Yes, it is true the universe is expanding, and as millions of years pass by, distances between worlds will extend, planets will freeze, and composite structures will change or evolve differently.

Intellectual minds of this current age, though, will soon state they desire specifics, answers to equations, and new information, but they are not ready. All must strive—if that is their academic goal—to discover the truth.

Remember, I am everything, and as we are all one, you are too. Therefore, 'matter' contracts and expands, but this is simply my heartbeat, and my breath. Do not picture a human heart but try to imagine the source and power of creation instead ... the pulse of life itself.

Please comprehend; all the billions of galaxies and solar systems are a minute part of me, so it may seem natural for people to think humanity is infinitesimal, or even insignificant. This is not the case because of your divinity. You are all these things too. You are I and I am you, no division ... wholeness. Therefore, you can know everything your 'need' requires if it is in truth, love, and light.

So, be positive and kind in your actions, thoughts, and words. Hold dear the faith in yourself, for then you sustain the same in me. Do not forget me, but hold me close in all of your endeavours. Do not be afraid, or fear will eat away your conscience and the ability to live in harmony and peace.

Overall, you can try to learn and question everything far beyond the Earth, but ultimately, your direct route to me is not from the exterior, but through the interior. Therein lies your greatest mystery, and the most beautiful discovery and answer. I am willing you and waiting for you. Know yourself and you will know me, as I love and care for you all. Amen.

LESSON 44:
NATURE

As I am closer than near, I know when you are 'still' and ready to receive the next lesson. Remember, like a child waiting for the teacher to begin, one must be prepared to open their heart and mind in order to accept what you need, without those exterior barriers of illusion and confusion so often discussed before.

In fact, this confirms a process is taking place, both within and out, because when energy and levels of light resonate at the same pitch and frequency, they bring the abilities you possess to the surface of the self, illuminating and shining in all directions.

Once this occurs, many spiritual and ethereal beings combine, ensuring the resulting connections take place. A knock-on effect transpires to alleviate the recipient's blockages in their chakras, enabling them to experience higher energies, which resonate and pulsate at greater speeds than their physical body currently resides.

I explain this to you now, as many souls have drawn close to you. You may or may not sense them, but this is not a task or issue for you within this process, either. The important thing is the effort one makes to partake, participate, share, and freely give the love communicated to you all. I am not concerned regarding the business side of producing these books but wish to reflect true comparisons between you all as human beings, with what you can see and feel all around you.

I am talking about the world in which you live, and the 'life' upon the Earth as you currently perceive it within nature. With information from your guides, you have already noted parts of this discussion in the earlier books—Pathway, and Deliverance of Love, Light and Truth. Therefore, we will now take this a step further, so those hearts who are opening up their true selves can expand and help others find their own truth too.

At first, most take those small baby steps, as if attending nursery school, but they evolve and flourish by receiving higher education, if, or when appropriate for them to do so. Tonight, as you sit and gaze through the window once more, leaves upon the trees sway and blow in the wind. Flowers, which are in full bloom, also dance within the breeze as the breath of life washes over them.

Sometimes, even at this time of year, one or two falls to the ground, disappearing from view, but because your earthly senses cannot see or touch them, do they cease to exist? Of course not ... and likewise, if two lovers or friends are miles apart, or a parent becomes separated from their child, does a connection end? Do their feelings dissipate, become diluted, fading into oblivion? No.

There are clear similarities existing between nature and 'human nature', but there are also vast differences. People may consider these are obvious comparisons to make, but if this were the case; the world in which you live would be a cleaner, safer, and a much brighter place to live.

Every soul can realise their true potential, though latent abilities can remain suppressed and withdrawn because of a loss of innocence, and the stress and decay of one's thoughts, words, and deeds. As such, the road to enlightenment, bliss and a permanent state of being can be as easy or as difficult as you make it. The source of your difficulties lies not in others, but in the 'self' and self-denial.

Indeed, humanity often hinders itself in pursuing impermanent desires and pleasure, but these only bring transitory feelings of fulfilment. Just as a leaf or flower petal falls away, it soon discolours as its beauty fades, and becomes part of the background (resembling the cycle of birth, life, and so-called death), and yet the essence remains. As time passes, this is re-nourished and blooms into another form, like your bodily incarnations, over many millennia.

Your task and goal are therefore to shine while you are currently here, and this must be in truth, with love and compassion. Therefore, during this embodiment, you can find bliss, and your impermanent state will be no more. Please understand, help and guidance will always be there for every being and soul.

You as the 'child', take these steps yourself, and in doing so, I will watch you crawl, kneel and stand, like a parent who oversees their offspring ... so walk toward the love that beckons you. Upon achieving this first real task, those who are present share smiles, laughter, and joy.

Compare this scenario with all who embark and step upon their new path unto me, for I am only a reflection of your true self. Do not fear, for I am within and by your side, and on your road of light I will protect and guide you through what you believe are your 'good' and 'bad' times ... and I will nurture you so your light shines like a star both near and far.

Right now, as the cloud and dark shadows begin to clear—in the sky—a brightness and clarity beam towards you. In this process, there is a removal of doubt and despair, and your life will be rich in contentment and peace.

Remember, it is important to understand, your seasons of change will be constant, just like nature. Therefore, you need to be adaptable, intuitive and go with the flow of your inner feelings and thoughts. Of course, I do not mean you should only ever consider your own, but make sure all you do is in the name of love, and with the foresight and action of true human values.

Lastly, I will relate what is flashing through your consciousness and mind. You think of nature's beauty, as well as its destructive power ... well appreciate the 'elementals' of earth, air, water and fire magnify life in all its glory, and also death.

So, energy ranging from the sublime and beautiful rainbow to the volcano's fire and brimstone ... and from the pure clear water of the sea to the tornado or hurricane from hell, are all events and occurrences which evolve from what is consumed and emitted (energy) from everyone who lives upon the impermanent plane. It is no more complicated or difficult to comprehend than this.

It has been, and always will be, essential to try to live in peace and harmony, with gratitude to and for Mother Earth who sustains your body. When you live in truth with nature, you will realise all life is one, and by doing so, every action leads to a positive and negative reaction. Therefore, balance is a key for stability and in being still, you can nurture your own true nature within. Amen.

LESSON 45:
BEING 'STILL' IN A WEB OF LIFE

Welcome, once again. Please understand, the depths of one's heart may reveal an abyss of uncertainty and doubt, or, in contrast, amazing peace and bliss. Therefore, while you seek and search within yourself, you can grow and learn much more than you believe was ever possible. Do you desire and really wish this, or are you afraid of what you will discover of your true self?

Simply being aware of the choices you are making (and their resulting actions), will all have an effect upon yourself. Regarding your goals and aspirations, people experience anxiety and frustration by deeming them as good, bad, or indifferent, but this not only influences your own way and path, but those of others who are close by and (seemingly), far away too.

In fact, your thoughts, words, and deeds enable such seeds to be sown and nurtured, allowing real growth and fulfilment. On the other hand, perhaps they will flounder, with one's hopes, dreams and wishes swirling inside the heart … like a feather, carried upon a gust of wind with no resting place. Remember, roots of a tree flourish with soil and water, and likewise, your strength of conviction and character can ground you and set you gently in place, where you can then contemplate and become still.

As I have stated on numerous occasions, this helps you reflect the truth both 'within' and out, to shine like a beacon, instead of a tiny spark or ember. Realise too, your divinity is a living flame of my love and light, of such beauty and majestic brilliance, these words cannot portray.

Countless souls and beings across many eras of history (and through vast planes and dimensions of energy), dampen their essence and divine spark because of unbalanced karma. Nonetheless, do not feel time is running out, though it is vital for you to rekindle the fire in order to expand in both wisdom and knowledge.

Through kindness and love, you can share with those who open their own hearts and minds, helping others to grow and know who they are and what they will become. Destiny is truth—and truth is destiny—and currently, you cannot mature spiritually or consciously without the experience of being in human 'form'. Please understand, through one's journey over many lifetimes (and the endeavours of mind and heart), piece by piece, the darkness of 'ego' and the lower self shall fall away.

You are all connected by strands of light and love,
While a soul is never 'born', from within or up above.
So, you yearn and try to search, from both heart and then your mind,
But I reveal you're so much more ... not alone or one of a kind.

Like the spider's web vibrating, upon and in the wind,
Fragments of life are 'captured', so do you think that you have sinned?
Yes, nourishment for one, and maybe fear and pain another,
While the experience is for all, of this you now discover.

In the centre it connects, as each link then forms a line,
A web of life to live ... in truth and you'll be fine.
Because energy is forever and this cannot be changed,
Only those who do not learn ... will think it all in vain.

Think of it right now, upon a cold and frosty morn,
It glistens and it glows, as the Sun begins to warm.
Frozen elements they do cling, from the deep and dead of night,
Or a quiet pause of stillness, do you long to now take flight?

For peace and now this truth, will melt all those hardened thoughts,
Captured by frames of time, you had believed they could be bought.
Not by money or material, or any false and earthbound pleasure,
The golden centre of all life ... I reveal as your true treasure.

So, know you are not trapped ... or enclosed to be passed by,
For growth and understanding, means the higher you can fly.
With knowledge now move on, and glow brightly as the 'Son',
Live eternally in peace, forever you and I as one.

Amen.

LESSON 46:
EACH A 'SUN' – WITH FREE WILL

Dear children of love and light, my peace and truth remain with you always, no matter where you are or whatever time of day or night. In fact, they will not diminish or fail, as I never stop to pause and reflect, even though people think or believe I do. Remember, you cannot be alone even when you rest or sleep, whether you travel into the deepest cavern, or stand upon the highest mountain, because we are 'one', always and forever.

For the many though, life exists only through the body—and consider it for simply living—but if you were to search inside yourself, you would realise this is a very singular and trivialising train of thought. Each of you must develop from within and expand your hearts and minds.

Please appreciate this is universal; and 'connections' between you all can never expire—or be extinguished—as I am everything, and always will be. Understand too, there is no greater force or energy, which subsequently recognizes and leads you towards your own knowledge and wisdom you require.

Only through division can confusion and darkness rain in. However, you can defuse and block all ills and decay with such simplicity—through your love. This is not always easy, especially in the face of provocation and illusion, but by trusting in yourself and me, you can achieve anything.

Every task you set, and each soul you seek to assist, are all part of me. Therefore, you can tap into untold wealth, not of materialism or a coveted nature, but the most important ingredient imaginable ... the universal life force of the love and light deep inside your soul. The divinity I speak of lives in everything. All you have to do is to recognize this, and through your faith and trust, achieve those goals you need and seek. Only human thoughts and actions create a false mystery and provide the same misguided voices who dispel the truth.

You can diffuse this by—and with—positive thoughts of love, and by doing so, not only do you expand the precious light from within, but you also help those who cannot see reality. In time, the entire world will know the difference between fact and fiction, and each person can grow if they choose to do so. Remember, utilise no pressure or exterior influences to coerce another. Someone may believe this can work, but when they deny the truth, it simply clouds the mind and heart.

Across the world, some think it is acceptable to force people into behaving a certain way by removing their freewill, so those involved cannot take a course of action of their own making. To deny choice brings negativity and its own consequences, but ultimately, even souls who lose sight of the truth must take the right path.

Therefore, when someone denies the acceptance of one's reality, is this right or wrong? Well, a soul can come across these options at any time, and therefore the decision to grow is forever each your own, but I will always encourage you to grasp the opportunities to shine your light. And, as your love is the key; you can place it in the door of your heart to reveal everything you could ever wish for, or you could simply dismiss this sweet, gentle calling of the teacher and master (within and out) ... and walk away.

Remember, this is your own choice and desire because you create, send, digest, and share the light. Indeed, you are each unique, so I advise you to bear witness to your own truth—but this will only occur when you view with the heart, mind, and soul in unison.

For example, if you were to gaze upon the burning sun, are you able to recognize its source and power, or do you squint and close your eyes at its brightness and warmth? True vision will enable you to perceive and grow with everything mentioned today, as you cannot survey its beauty and its magnificent patterns of energy.

Indeed, not only does the Sun sustain you with heat, light, and life upon the Earth, it is also a beacon, a symbol of universal power, a star ... one of many, both near and far. Realise there are countless Suns in many galaxies and solar systems, though you can only observe these from within yourself when aligned with the truth.

The peace it sends is a 'symbol', way beyond your billions of years of evolution, and day or night it is continuous, just like my love. Ask yourself, if you do not see the Sun in the sky, would you believe it exists? In addition, just as the grey and dark mists rise and fall within Earth's atmosphere, could they similarly cloud your true vision ... feel this message inside your heart, and you will know it's true meaning.

You are all part of the eternal 'Son' and of the Sun, too. As such, you are each a sun, so do not stay in the shade or hide in the darkness. Walk free and be free to share and illuminate your pathway ahead of you.

Try to guide all those opening their eyes and hearts for the first time, because, just like new-born children, they may cry, but it takes no force or pain for them to 'realize' their rebirth, for truth is gentle. In addition, love is so immense, and by sharing and giving, they will see. There is no need to push or shove, for a few words, a smile, a thought or even a prayer can help each soul flower and bloom at their own recognition. It is not for you to decide, as I have mentioned many times before.

You are all segments of the puzzle, a unique jigsaw. As you are all one, you form the overall picture, and are therefore already complete. You need to view this as being more than one-dimensional, and not through your eyes, which attempt to tell you what you can or cannot see.

Know that much work is to be done, whether above, below, within or out, and wherever you live too, but you are never alone, so live and shine the light forever. Soar high and let your love flow, for you will never fail. Be still now, and at peace, until you are ready to release the light once again through the words of a loving pen. Amen.

LESSON 47:
LIGHT AND SIGHT TO NEW LEVELS

You may be able to open your eyes and look both far and wide, but when you try to gaze upon things close by, you can become unfocused, unable to bear witness to what lies before you. Therefore, physical sight can perceive all, and yet see nothing ... so to, one's perspective of life can lie shrouded by clouds of illusion, which dull the mind, and place a shield around your heart.

For this reason, those who do not wish to express their love from within will observe no further than the boundary they themselves set. Or, even worse if they withdraw into darkness, ultimately lose their true insight. In essence, looking through the eyes of the body can reveal a tissue of lies ... but if you seek from a point of truth, you grow and understand that we never part.

Please appreciate, while it is possible to view light from all directions, one can only recognize it with love, which is the power, the bond and the radiance of divine energy that nourishes and sustains your soul. I am the light, and everything emanates from me, so you would think all life would comprehend this.

However, this is not the case, because the eyes of the mind, body and spirit are not always functioning as one, and hence they display blurred vision through distorted lenses. People search inside vast clouds of darkness, but if they were to cleanse and wipe the mist away from the lens of their hearts—which is the centre of all beings and souls—you expose the truth.

The way to do this is not new, or only for the few. You all have the ability to experience and become encompassed by my eternal radiance, so try to reveal your own brilliance from within. Indeed, this is an open door, which lies ajar and is never far ... because we reside in each other.

You do not need to look beyond the horizon or climb the highest mountain; you do not need to cross a deep ocean or continent to find my loving, outstretched hand. When you genuinely search, you find me, and at the appropriate time, 'ascend', as can all humankind.

This message (or lesson) exists from, through and to light, for you are the light, so do not wear darkened bands around the eyes of your true self anymore. You must also cast aside the shadows of doubt to walk and hold hands of love who exists in all places and remove those feelings of hate and acts of sin—and let love, light and truth restore your true vision to 'win'. All life deserves an eternity within the light, and so the victory is yours to grasp. (Remember though, it is often a sacrifice to live and learn and sometimes yearn for answers you desperately seek to find).

Understand that you are me and I am you, and together we are all one of a kind. You are each a feather, which forms a wing Remember, upon the dove of peace, and our love is the other, the partner and the key, enabling you to take flight and fulfil your destiny. Therefore, fly high, higher than you thought or believed was possible. Discover the truth in all you do, then all your dreams they will come true. So…

> The musical notes that flow, above you and below,
> Move like many souls, but which way do they go?
> Will they sing and chime, into peace of the divine,
> Or do they drift into the mist, perhaps forever and all time?
>
> With a search it now begins, even though the door was open,
> To lead you now all 'in', to bestow and not be broken.
> A reward for those who have, revealed the truth unto themselves,
> That life is love and knowing, the 'I' and then the self.
>
> Because inside of you is light, and you're so welcome please don't hide,
> Eternal lives are there for all, climb aboard upon this ride.
> So … gain ascension and a level, of love and joy, no pain,
> A sacrifice and your task, but is it cruel and all in vain?
>
> In truth no need to worry, for you are overseen,
> To pastures rich and new, or before where you have been.
> There is something true, in every voice or smile and thing,
> Revealed through love and light, pure hearts now out of sin.
>
> And so, the choice is truth, and yours alone to make,
> And in the peace you ask, 'What is it at stake?'
> But only you can then, define your goal and path that's set,
> Though for me you were not born, as we've already met.
>
> And from the burning Sun, you're everlasting in my love,
> So do not ask where from, or now below or up above.
> For you it's only just, and just it only is,
> Therefore, do not ever worry; a soul's choice is one for bliss.

Now those rays fall from within, and also then without,
Please do not ever cry … or plead or cast a doubt.
For the goodness you each do, will see you shine, and all come through,
As love contains it 'all', and that includes both me and you.

Then you'll see the 'Son', and ask the why, the how and when,
Open hands so now just write, with love and I both through this pen.
You freewill to go and share, to give all from your true heart,
Tell all who want to listen, that we are 'one' and do not part.

Yes 'one' and both in time, and for each and all dimension,
Revealed then is my love, it is for you and not just Heaven.
The peace, the love and light, that is forever there contained,
Is free and you are all, from despair or hate and pain.

So now, it is your moment, to truly see the light,
Within and also out, each day and every night.
Just go and make a wish, for all that's said and true,
For in my light please know I love you, so don't feel down or sad or blue.

Amen.

LESSON 48:
PARALLEL LINES

As you sit and become 'still' together, recognizing love from the 'Son', you'll grow and continue to learn as one. After all, even while you live on the physical plane, your true essence and divinity inside you—which is without such restrictions—can therefore receive and send parallel lines of communication and love upon numerous dimensions.

However, even though nothing is separate or divided, people call a soul as a fragment or spark of me, which is why so many of you ask, "How can this be?" Once again, it appears inevitable that the devotee, disciple, or the inquirer will always wish to know the how, why, and wherefore, too.

Well, perhaps the answer is in the question itself, and therefore my reply is to be still. This way, you will comprehend being part of everything. It justifies the truth and desire for personal growth, understanding your very existence, and of all things imaginable too.

Please understand, truth flows in many ways and forms, though some think it arrives from somewhere in the abyss. When you take this conception too far, you twist reality, because 'out there' means nothing more than going within oneself and vice versa. Remember, everything is whole, and yet as life co-exists upon every vibration/energy in time and space, they may seem separated from each other, but are, in fact, complete. Division only appears in the mind, because love and light was, are, and always will be, the same, universal and eternal.

As such, the gifts you share in different ways and means—through the transference and love from me (I am I)—are special. It is vital, therefore, that you believe that any method of communication is above or below another. This can be hard to accept sometimes, especially when your heart requests so many things, or longs for the opportunity to experience the joy through me in some other shape or form. You can compare this with your earthly senses. For example, would a blind person wish they were deaf, in order they could see? If you cannot feel or touch—would you prefer, you could not taste instead?

The way you each develop is for your own individual growth and purpose. On the outside, someone may appear more holy, gentle, and caring, yet this can be deceptive, so the most important aspect is truth, which flows to and from the heart. Everything else is secondary.

Returning to the examples above, does the 'channel' or vessel yearn to express itself in other ways? Remember, each step and learning process is for the moment, so move forward and grow with these gifts by learning to appreciate and share them, which can only enhance what you are receiving and giving from your heart.

You are all equal, and inside you are the same, made from love ... to expand love. Physical appearances suggest your differences, but it is your own perception of such that separates and causes the divisions within your societies, countries, and the world.

The core of all souls is identical, and in every galaxy and element of light, only the awareness of the truth is different. This, together with a soul's comprehension of its own existence, creates individuality and character, which comes across as being unique and so diverse from each other.

Indeed, if everyone resembled each other—in physical presence and body —then what I have given to you in order to experience and grow in countless and complex ways would be lost. Appreciate nothing can erase the freedom and individuality of the soul deep within, so even though one may think or believe I deny this, once again, it is only the person's environment which gives this impression.

Comprehend those external influences can appear to restrict you, and yet within the soul, there are no barriers or any lock and key. So, the planes and energy of different dimensions are accessible through the spiritual gifts I give you, but I am the truth and the light beyond comprehension, and you can change these.

Do not fear what I say but understand these parallel lines of vibration and resonance are simply 'you' and these shine through your own divinity. So, if you crave for truth, does the desire to bask within the light overwhelm you? Please do not let it, because balance and equalization are important.

Many will know the following phrases, 'as above, so below' and 'you can only learn to the level that you have reached', as well as, 'too much, too soon' and 'do not run before you can walk'. You are souls, but like children, need to understand guidance always materialises at the right time in your life.

Remember, you can and must express freewill in love and peace, yet find balance in your physical world with the higher vibrations you seek. Everything is compatible and interlinked with destiny, karma, and life. Humankind needs to recognize this and release their fears of under- achievement, failure, and death of the body. Consider your soul is universal, and the universe is your soul.

Simplified further, your soul and life are love, and every ingredient, atom, cell, structure, infrastructure, and level of vibration are one. All are whole; you are complete. Everything you could ever possibly need and seek is inside yourself.

In a similar vain to what I discussed earlier, when you cannot see with your physical eyes, does it mean you cannot witness the truth? If you have no ears, can you not hear me? Is a broken heart unable to love? Only fear and a false manifestation can misconstrue this because all you could ever ask for lives within you already, so you must learn to trust in the love and light to soar and take flight.

Decisions are always yours to make, and no one can take these away from you. Nothing can prevent you from your growth but yourself ... through self-denial, and those boundaries and barriers you put in place. One's choice is therefore to accept—or deny—the truth.

I ask in times of pain or anguish that you do not despair and say you do not care. This will only compound what you may be trying to release on a much deeper or karmic level. Remember, those in perilous situations should not give up hope or just accept the situation as their fate. I understand this is often difficult to comprehend and accept this entwined scenario, though.

To help you, I ask you to imagine a hostage, separated from family and loved ones, which is a situation manifesting many times across the Earth. Is this 'experience', this learning process, for the hostage, their family, or for those who seem to be in control ... the 'captors'? Well, try to understand and recognize they have no real power!

A situation can be like this for many reasons, and far beyond the reasoning of those who imagine they can influence and misshapen freewill. Universal law is holy, full of love and experience. Realise no matter how painful the experience, this can be overcome with trust and faith, so look forward to the light. Yes indeed, any situation will turn out right, for the meaning of these things will become clearer as the heart becomes purer.

Appreciate that love always prevails, even in the most desperate situations. It cannot diminish, become erased, or forgotten, when through and from inside your soul. For now, rest this pen and take flight, knowing your heart is always open to the truth. Amen.

LESSON 49:
GUILT ... OR SHAME?

Even though you feel I had to wait—for you to pick up the pen—please do not think you have offended or troubled me in terms of time or my patience. In fact, these are trivial to me, as I exist within the when, where, and the why of all things, and am therefore with you always. So, as you write the beginning of this passage of text, what was your initial reaction? Is there a sense of guilt or shame in one's life? You do not need to tell me, because I know your heart and soul in the same way I know all beings and every element of life throughout creation.

Please comprehend; the title and lesson are important at this stage of the book, for its purpose is to bring specific thoughts and feelings to the forefront of every mind regarding their own lives and surroundings, as well as those who reside far away too.

Indeed, many assume I must be angry or annoyed with them, but by now, every soul should know this is not, and never will be, the case. That very thought is simply the reflection of what one actually thinks, as I do not judge any of you. Therefore, one must follow my example, difficult as it may be, especially when faced with provocation, persecution, threats, or stress, which often materialise within the cocoon of general living.

Still, humanity has to overcome these difficulties in order to move forward in love and truth. Realise such problems occur because you imagine they take place with some sort of inevitability, or even believe it is your own fault too. However, because the world is uniquely connected and linked in a vast number of ways, this is an incorrect viewpoint.

Appreciate I bear witness to everything upon the 'earth-plane' and recognize how global views affect you all in a positive or negative manner. Nearly every major event, which ranges from your current world financial crisis to so-called natural disasters, all seem to grip and squeeze you, which can shake you to the core.

Understand, too, the problem with most governments—and those who assume they are in power—are their thoughts and beliefs in their own importance, imagining separateness and division, which eventually leads the ego in the desire to control. Until you all come to terms with the concept and essence of being whole, negative traits will enter the consciousness and attempt to pick away at love, light, and the good so many of you do.

Consequently, in times of struggle … pleas and cries ring out, piercing me like a dagger. Of course, this expresses speech only—for I am beyond all such things—while emotions become magnified tenfold when true pain or joy flows from the body, mind, or soul. It is vital to filter false anxiety, especially concerning the loss of any material possessions or anything else in the impermanent world.

Within the current economic climate, people across the globe shout or scream as the price of their shares decrease or falls sharply, sending them into a blind rage. A similar reaction occurs when the value of people's homes drops by thousands of pounds, dollars, euros or whatever the currency in the country where you live.

Indeed, fear grips nation after nation, and as one country's wealth decreases, they fall down, one after the other, like dominoes. Panic sets in, stirred and raised by media speculation and so forth, and yet people talk of their assets dwindling, even though they still live in a house, place food on the table and wear shoes upon their feet.

Please understand, when the eyes of the soul, heart and mind are fully open as one, you will see through these events and face the truth. If you outstretch your hand to help a stranger, you will know the truth, and to realise your neighbour is part of you, you experience the truth.

As people discuss the cost of oil and fuel for their cars and homes, they gave though little thought or gratitude to the host and the giver of such things. I am talking about Mother Earth where your physical resides. She provides the world with everything your body needs to function, like the crops to nourish you and the rain to quench your thirst.

Indeed, the planet is so beautiful and amazing, but in recent years, people were oblivious to her vulnerability and condition. Therefore, instead of debating 'uncertain times', there are more important questions such as "How can we protect the Earth and life upon her?"

Well, the thoughts of a single person can help to change the many. Therefore, by tending one's own garden—your character and personality—whereby you live and nurture true human values, the seeds of love will sprout further afield. You could picture vast acres of barren soil (or weeds), but through perseverance and understanding of your fellow man's needs, they become full of light and spiritual growth. Like a patchwork quilt, we can sow together them to form a collective layer of hope and peace, covering the world in a blanket of love.

I now state, in returning to the beginning of this lesson, do you feel any guilt or shame? Have you been true to yourself this day? Were you able to help another soul in your society? Did an opportunity pass you by … and if so, does it now make you want to weep and cry?

Remember, one great factor you can foster within your life is contentment, because this powerful trait dispels attachment and fear. However, with food in your stomach, do you think of those who hunger? If your throat is moist or wet from water, do you think of those who thirst? When friends come to help you in your hour of need, can you spare a thought for those who are lonely, lost, or sad? So ... please try to be content in the areas of your life that truly matter.

Don't be afraid or worry about doom and gloom but share your love and goodwill. Your hearts can bask in the glory of the 'Son' every day, just as the Sun will shine and rain falls somewhere around the globe. This I promise, so sharing the Earth's resources should be a priority ... fairly and evenly, and with care and compassion.

If you can believe and hope all beings can be true to themselves, one day, this will happen. Please do not sink deeper into yourself, so that your light lies in shadow. You are a living flame, and I wish you to move forward—even one small step at a time—in order to shine more brightly.

Your illumination will make others lie in warmth and serenity, and each soul will realise I join them in an unbroken cord of love. Some may disagree, citing any chain is only as strong as the weakest link, but I ask you to forget those of the impermanent world, as they cannot compare.

Remember, you are I as I am you, and any so-called fragment or 'child' of light contains the same power and strength. Nothing ... absolutely nothing, can ever break my bond to you, for you are all the fabric of my heart and existence.

I implore you to grow and fulfil your destiny. Release any guilt or shame trailing behind you right now in your lives. Help the love that lies beside you —or even on the other side of the world—by being true and kind in all you do, think, and pray.

You can all change the way every nation act and reacts with its neighbour, if you only believe in yourself and each other, and if you do, you also believe in me. Remember, at the start of this lesson, I stated you are never alone, so I am with you, always and forever. Amen.

LESSON 50:
WAR AND PEACE, LOVE AND HATE

Welcome. Let me start this lesson by explaining I neither condemn, nor condone, your own thoughts, words, and deeds upon the physical plane. All action, and therefore its results, are brought to bear yourselves ... it has been, and always will be, this way for each one of you.

As this is the case, you possess the ability to enhance or degenerate life and everything around you, which is displayed through the mind, body, or spirit. We can deem these as three separate elements of the 'I', but they are one, because they make you complete. Knowing this, we will now begin with War and Peace.

Ever since human beings roamed the Earth—and before speech even began—man, woman, and child could live in either harmony or conflict. Indeed, throughout history, people with different cultures and ideals reside together within villages, towns, cities, or countries the world over. With all the technology and experience of today, nothing has changed, and in this respect, time has made no difference at all. So how does war start? Who initiates heartache and pain, and why does anger and hatred seem to endure?

Well, in order to explain many things, it might be easier to take the mind back to those childhood days of innocence, for even as a child, one could display aspects of their character that usually remain hidden. Children will often shout or argue a point of view such as, "That's mine!" Alternatively, "I'm not sharing it!" Many will accuse me of being too simplistic here, but you all need to rethink about who, what and why you exist—or more importantly, co-exist—amongst every form of life.

Remember, truth is simple, and therefore, I will give no one an inferiority complex through a supposed lack of understanding. If you can unblock the past, which leads to your 'present,' this will guide you to your future.

War can start when two minds, or rather two hearts, do not meet or share within the truth of who they are. This then splinters into greed, jealousy, pride, hate, and thoughts of power over another, which resemble needles that pierce and blind true sight, casting eyes into shadow, doom, and gloom.

The results of which make people cry out to me from the depths of their despair, "Why did you let this happen, God? How could you take them away from me? When did you stop caring for us?" Every tear and prayer I hear, see, sense, and feel with all that I am. Nothing is lost or diluted, whether in joy or pain — as I am you and you are I—so why should anyone suffer? For what reasons should a country or nation be ravaged, and war torn?

Time and time again, we revert to one's karma, this cause and effect, balance and imbalance, light, and darkness, and you already know the reasons why things happen. Finite details are not required, for you do not need me to recite examples of conflict after conflict ... and war after war, throughout Earth's history. What is more important right now is for every individual to open their heart and soul to truth, love, and light.

True peace comes to those who do not desire anyone or anything, and those that dilute and dissolve their ego find inner peace more quickly, and subsequently find their higher self. This brings illumination and recognition of their own divinity and me. Once you recognize this, understanding new knowledge becomes easier, life is more fulfilling, and you can blossom into the soul you strive to be.

I listen when people say, "I want peace, let there be peace, bring peace to him, her, or this or that country" etcetera, but what is it actually wished for ... comfort, joy, and stillness? On the other hand, is it for others so they can find help, shelter, protection, food, or water? Well, peace encompasses all things, so when nothing is required, peace reigns.

This will happen when you realise that tranquillity is within yourself, and then by linking with your neighbour, family, friends, or even a stranger, you form real chains of love—the strongest force imaginable. This cannot be broken by time or distance. Interestingly, while memories can fade, the imprint upon the heart and soul is eternal, and therefore, no matter what incarnation you find yourself, you can discover the reality and live eternally within me.

Realise the answers can be found within the questions. The 'back and forth' sensation is your own battle you embark upon, and these feelings and intuition are the gauges, swinging from truth and love via illusion and hate. Every one of you constantly wages your own inner war to find peace.

The hatred, which can ooze from every cell of the body, is negativity and confusion, and must be erased. Remember too, hate brings anguish, anguish leads to fear, fear leads to stress, and stress is 'disease' (ill at ease), and ultimately, death of the body. It is also representing the blindness to another's love and joy, and like a reflection within a strange mirror at a funfair ... it distorts and contorts the true image of light itself. It detracts you away from the rays of the Sun—and Son—which beam the radiance both inside and out.

Therefore, starting today, from this minute of the hour, you can change. You can make a difference to your own life and soul and destiny, and from the alterations you make, you can effectively cast light far beyond your heart and the walls of your home, to wherever that may be.

Never despair or fear any situation. I am not saying for anyone to be ruthless or careless in any action one takes, but request you find your own direction—in and to the truth. Remember, I am nearer than near, and I will never leave you, even through your worst pain or greatest joy, for I am with and within you. Believe in me, as I always believe in you … as we are 'one' forever, and I will lead you into bliss. Amen.

LESSON 51:
HAPPINESS

Happiness ... is it for the many, only the few, or just for you? Of course, many people of all ages and from different walks of life will strive in the pursuit of some kind of elusive pleasure. In fact, it does not matter whether you are old and grey, or even an infant, opening their eyes from another re-birth to the physical plane of energy and vibration.

Indeed, there is an inbuilt sense or ill-fated burning desire within each of you, which haunts and casts its shadow over almost every thought during daily acts of work, rest, and play. These incorrect notions are because of craving anything or everything, which could be material, emotional or physical, but nonetheless, this false and sometimes dangerous illusion comes primarily from the mind.

Therefore, to dig deeper into this scenario, let us take a child who craves not only comfort, warmth, and food, but who will also display a continual 'want' which seems to take hold over their whole being. Ask any parent who carries their kith and kin through any toy or sweet shop—as some try to justify their actions—"I bought this because it made them happy", but this is a temporary solution, and will never fulfil their one true need.

Over the years, one hopefully grows and matures through adolescence, adulthood, and retirement, and eventually one may realise they were tested frequently by desire or greed. Do not become confused while striving to achieve personal goals and ambitions if conducted from—or in—truth. Subsequently, if your labour and hard work bear fruits in your life and domain, these are just rewards ... of which there is nothing wrong at all.

Only when the attachments of such take hold of the heart will they lead to feelings of inadequacy and disharmony, and discontent. People look at their spouse, home, car, neighbours, and relative's etcetera, and may wish they had made different choices, and so the expression, 'not being satisfied with their lot' now springs to mind.

Before the reader believes this lesson or message sounds like a lecture or a telling off, please do not feel this way, as every image and thought these words create inside yourself is provided to reflect and share the truth. If it were not so, you would have placed this book on one side by now.

I only reiterate these things to highlight the unnecessary striving that is deep set within the psyche of humankind, whereas all souls need only one goal, which is to return to your true home and place of residence inside my heart. This is where you will find your real happiness and pure bliss, and you cannot find this by buying the latest gadget, car, new home or through a continual change of partner. Remember, soul to soul or heart to heart 'connections' are permanent. Everything else upon the 'earth-plane' will dissipate and fade—inner happiness does not.

A comparison with false pleasures is like a stone tossed into a clear pool of water, causing concentric rings to ripple outwards ... at first, they are clearly seen, but soon disappear from view as if they never happened at all. This represents the weight of a fictitious hope, which disappears, sinking into the depths of your heart. In complete contrast, when two people are in love, they can remember their first kiss, when they held hands, and even where, and what time it was when they met!

Therefore, you could say love is happiness, and happiness is love. Now try to remember being in love yourself, or at least recall the deepest, strongest bond for a person, pet, place, or even something you have seen. If you could multiply this by infinity, then this is bliss, true peace, and contentment.

So how can you be happy? Is it when you have the brand-new car, getting promotion, moving home, or being with a new partner? No, because, as I reiterate, all are impermanent and form attachment. To recognise one's freedom, you do not need to give up these things, you only need to change the importance and priority of them within your life.

Simply trust in yourself and in me. Have strength and conviction in your faith too, and with hope in all you do, your confidence in your own ability to overcome hardship and transgressions shall materialise. In time, you can control and change your state of mind as soon as it tries to trick and behold you, then you will see and become 'lighter' in all your thoughts and words and deeds.

Every day and night, you can make a difference. Your vibration and energy levels will increase so much, you will resonate and send love from within, not only to those close by but also those who touch your own heart both near and afar.

I understand sceptics will say happiness is a state of mind, yet I explain your true contentment lies outside of your mind, for without it; you do not need to conjure up images or control feelings of desire. People can relate to the words, "I want happiness" and "I want peace", but as I explained before, if you take away the 'I'—which relates to ego—and the want, which is the desire—they leave you with the goal and the truth.

I say to you, push aside the false prison bars captivating every thought process, because the door was already open, even when you thought you had needed a new key. Your heart can set the mind free, guiding it from the cell and false barriers you yourself erected. Nothing can stop you and nothing can hurt you, for you are I and I am you. This alone will bring you home, to be eternally happy ... and happily eternal. For now, be at peace and rest, God bless. Amen.

LESSON 52:
THE CHOICE

Welcome to all light and life and love. Now, as you sit and become still once more, you ponder and hope for something special. Gratitude and humbleness also shine from your heart to touch mine, along with a truthful desire for the illumination of new insight, wisdom, and knowledge—which are indeed all special—but for whom does this also apply?

Well, a single sentence of this book can reignite the flame of truth within a soul, like a lightning bolt from the sky, but others, perhaps bewildered and confused, require more time to discover the inspiration to fulfil their goals, in whatever form that may be.

Therefore, when you become cognisant of my presence and voice—which echoes through your divinity—do your feelings change at all? I believe so, for you pursue and carry out your work of service willingly and eagerly, and if this were not the case, then the collation of this text would not have reached its second page.

Please appreciate; many inquisitive souls will look upon these pages for personal growth and understanding. They may even yearn inside their hearts to find a real purpose to their own lives. The list is endless, and yet these are the same, for ultimately everything is to, from, or for love. Every aspect and facet of light exists for this one reason, and nothing can alter, deceive, or even delay its outcome.

Therefore, only an individual can challenge his or herself where their destiny is concerned. Only the soul will comprehend its actions, it's freewill to adjust to the path of righteousness or self-denial. However, before one states I may be heavy-handed in my expressions, one must realise the lessons contained here are shared at a precise and particular point, and for every season.

In fact, we have spoken frequently—over the years—regarding time and its relevance on the 'earth-plane', and so the words you transcribe fall onto their appropriate page and space when required to do so. As such, for those who read or hear these words, you could start at the so-called beginning, and follow the subsequent flow of 'lessons', or you may even choose any one at random. Whatever takes place is because you need it. This same principle applies throughout your life, for everything exists for a reason, and has its place in the grand scheme of things.

Please understand, I planted the seeds for growth through and by your own efforts. Ultimately, you will recognize this, and so one's circumstances and situations in which you find yourself take place precisely when they are meant to, not when you want them to. Any path you choose, or a so-called positive or negative event, is for your higher good to balance karma, and lift your soul.

Remember, through trust, you live without fear, so do not be concerned or box yourself in with worries or doubts. These will only slow you down, preventing you from picking up pace towards self-realization. It is enough, therefore, to simply just 'be' ... in thought, word, and deed. Do not pretend to be someone who you are not, and do not feel you need to justify your existence to anyone or anything, in any place or dimension. You are who and what you are, and everything around you is temporary and of the mind's illusion.

You may even think of yourself as being a body with a soul, but it is the exact opposite—a soul within a body. You should also sense when your mind dictates to you, so if you become agitated by minor irritations or inconveniences, try to remember, you are as 'I am'.

Through knowledge and experience, you gain wisdom, in order to understand you are light and love, a resonance of divinity, so it is you—and only you—who can comprehend your own internal brilliance. An earthly mirror cannot see this, for that reflection is false, fleeting, and impermanent for the impermanent world. Therefore, the choice is your own, and you can make it right this second ... or deny it altogether.

With new thoughts flashing across the brain and mind, impulses, and signals swirl about, which causes you to think and wonder what this might be. Well, it is an appreciation that it does not matter where you are upon your quest and search and journey—or whatever level you or anyone else believe you are on—you must ask yourself whether you wish to progress or continue the old ways of living and being.

This day can be a start of something new and brilliant, which changes your life and those around you forever. Each day forthwith can be lived as if it was your last, with meaning, justification and one of hope and glory. Only you can limit love, which emanates from the kindness and peace pouring from your heart.

You can light the beacon of joy and faith by reigniting the spark of your soul's flame, to radiate and bloom with serenity and splendour, and majestic in both simplicity and grace. By your very nature, you will nurture those who will draw close to you, captivating them with a smile and guiding them with an open hand. All of this you can realise upon your path, only the choice remains to be seen.

Appreciate the importance in remembering this, but do not see it as a test I decree or set. As I am you and you are I, this was already in place, for there was no beginning and there shall be no end. The important decision you face is only current because of the way all souls have manifested and grown through time and experience. Your own freewill and karma created such a false sense of separation and illusion when there is none. You are all one, and nothing can alter or change this.

Therefore, no matter where you live or in what religion you follow or believe, find its truth and strength. I will never ask you to stop or deny your earthly heritage or practices, because you only need to walk the path of honesty, integrity, and to share your love.

If you do, then no persuasion, delusion, or any twist of fate can make you hurt anyone or anything. It is man and man alone who misconstrues or diverges from this road, to govern or hold power over another person or land. Within any sacred text or wisdom of heart, where does hate or anger decree to do such things? If these occur, it is then your freewill to uphold your true beliefs, so do not fear consequences … for I am with you always— in all ways.

Remember too; you grow and mature alongside those who share these words with open hearts and souls. Do not concern yourself or worry over where this work will be received, as this is not your priority, and never will be. Just trust in me, as I place my trust in you all.

Know the world is a beautiful place but is often cast into shadow and gloom through desperation and fear, even so, every soul can be the light expressed in eternal truth. Billions of you live there, but only temporarily … so honour yourselves by honouring each other. Live with human values and right conduct, which I bestow upon you inside and out.

With your heart, mind, and soul as one, you will clearly view the path ahead, which needs perseverance, fortitude, and endurance by all. Please also love the things you think cannot 'think' and wrap your arms around those who are less fortunate upon the earthly road you tread.

Feel, sense, and acknowledge me in the grass, flowers, trees, rivers, seas, mountains, sky, fire, earth, and the space beyond. Realise me within the stillness inside yourself, for here I reside with and for you, in order to guide you towards eternal bliss.

I shall never leave you and always love you. Your heart is my own, and your life can express the divinity that is truly you. Be at peace and complete your destiny ... knowing your dreams are my own, and I will help you to fulfil them all. We are one always and forever. Amen.

CONCLUSION—Part 1:
'GOD'S LOVE'

Unique, brilliant, majestic, all powerful and healing, it is all, and all is love. Reflect upon this statement and let it nourish the core of yourself and your 'self'.

You yearn and contemplate, perhaps worrying and dreading your life—and life's tasks—that you yourself have set (or have been laid down for you), but I say, just 'be'.

There is no commandment, instruction, or rule book for you to digest, read, or act upon. If you simply know yourself, your higher-self and soul, then all will work out exactly right ... every day and night.

Deem that the connection is to, from, up, down, behind, in front, sideways, within, and out ... as every route lead to God's love. Everywhere, yes in all places, and in all beings, is the love—which was not born—but given freely to all creation.

Realise that the sweetest smell and fragrance, the lightest touch, the brightest and most warm Sun (and Son), the freshest breeze, the bluest sky, the highest and most low vibration, and all forms of energy are all my love ... which is within and is everything. Therefore, rejoice, bask, feel, and truly be this love, too.

Acknowledge and be proud to have found and walk with love through the treadmill of life. Up the highest hills and your downward slopes, through your believed good and bad times, just follow, guide, and share love that is free for you all.

As you well know, a beating heart of the physical pumps its blood to all the organs of the body so that you can live the way you do. While this is so, my heart also beats the purest love to sustain and help you grow and know the truth of whom, what and why you are.

Hence, to feel my love and then acknowledge it leads to understanding, and the experience required for both the individual and group soul journeys. The emphasis is plain and simple and isn't complicated.

The best things in life are 'free'. This is truth and wisdom. These words can be a springboard to more joy and happiness that love contains, if only more of you believed in it. It is unrivalled, has no comparison and no equal. There is no division, it is 'all' and all is love.

A flower and a tree are all born from just one seed,
And the rays of the true Sun, are born out from deep need.
So, you bathe and are then engulfed, in peace and also love,
My power and grace, come from within and up above.

It is right and it is now, and it is by day and then by night,
So … discover and accept freely, and freely give out what is right.
No holding back, of what are the within and the without,
No laying still, a life of love, of which there is no doubt.

From roof tops or high mountains, those do seem to touch the sky,
No need to ever wonder, or cry out asking, 'Why?'
For you all have the gift, and the 'present' from my heart,
And 'one' forever is a promise … to never, ever part.

Amen.

CONCLUSION—Part 2:
'GO IN PEACE AND WITH FORGIVENESS'

In one hand, man has a gun and in the other an open heart. With one thought, he can break it, pierce it clean through … or he can mend it with kindness, compassion, and love.

Throughout the ages, there has been a power-struggle within the body, mind, and soul. This innate struggle manifests itself deep in the core of the 'self' and it surfaces on many planes of time and dimension.

The individual and the masses, both far and wide, can feel the effect of the so-called good and bad, light, and dark, love and hate, and so on and so forth. The light connects each one of billions and therefore every action has a reaction and recoil, an effect which can transform or digest the cause.

Every thought and word and deed that manifests has a minute or massive effect upon others around the world—and also within you, too. How does one perceive it? Can one control it? Do you judge it? All are questions with many answers, but simplicity is always the key.

If all souls did everything with peace and compassion, then there is no worry, anxiety, or concern. But how can this be acted out by the people, the governments, and the nations? The answer is easily and freely; it only needs to be tried. There is no magical potion or formula to follow other than the heart itself.

In your impermanent world today—in the climate of greed, envy, and desire—it can be so difficult, though only because your mind tells you it is. Only through new ways of believing, being, and acting whom and what you are can bring change. It is within this understanding that all—if they wish to —must alter their 'self'.

Every day contains the opportunities to alter—for the better—both within and out. Do not judge others, but be true to yourself, for all good deeds, actions, and reactions will spread and be seen by others with both physical and spiritual eyes.

Do not look for rewards … or of what is yours or mine. Simply have an open heart and soul and let your light shine like a beacon, attracting and sending out wave after wave of vibration energy with love, peace, and forgiveness.

Please do not be hard upon yourselves when you are weak, but acknowledge the fact that you have recognized it and move on … gaining strength in fortitude and perseverance. Others will see this new strength and become inspired and act according to their own heart and mind's perception.

You are never alone as I am the light, 'spirit', and love—and both the high and low, the in and out, time and no time, as well as space and no space. Indeed, all things are sent—and received—by me. They are seen or unseen, heard or unheard, perceived or ignored, accepted or denied, loved or unloved, touched or untouched, and sensed or not sensed.

In the spirit world—and in every dimension—please hope and pray for the truth, love, and light. For all things are here and here within, lies all things.

Remember who and what you really are and, by experiencing and living it in the physical, it will be mirrored back and forth, both inside and out of your soul. Being true to both yourself and others is all anyone can ask of you. If everyone can follow the love within their hearts, then all will forgive and find peace.

Do not attempt to find the differences between these last few words … as some will say, forgiveness and peace are separate, two unrelated things, yet they are not. I entwine them, encompassed like a pearl in a shell. It is when the hardened shell of hate opens—by the action of forgiveness—that truth, beauty, and the love of peace are made known to those that reveal and share it, as well as for those who receive it. This truth is for everyone … but those who acknowledge it all also 'will' it to happen.

Be still in the knowingness of this love and light. Try to open the outer casing of your own heart and expose the beauty of the completeness within. Let peace shine eternally from inside your heart's centre and soul. Let this be the truth and so fulfil your one true goal.

Finally, thank you for writing and conveying these precious words, David, from, to and beyond the heart. Until next time you sit and become 'still', love and light within the spirit realms and dimensions around you will be waiting. Your friends and 'family' who are from far and wide and through space and time *will* return on the wave and tide of love. I bless you all. Amen.

FURTHER READING

You will find your own guidance and inspiration every day, week, month, or year as nothing in life is ever by 'chance'. Each Lesson will simply be the most appropriate for your needs at that time, helping you to find inner peace and balance and your own spiritual education, growth and understanding. Here is a selection of my favourite books / authors and which I hope you will enjoy reading.

Sai Baba Gita-
The Way to Self Realization and Liberation in this age.
By Al Drucker
ISBN 0-9638449-0-3

Conversations with God
By Neale Donald Walsh
Book 1 - ISBN 0-340-69325-8
Book 2 - ISBN 0-340-76544-5
Book 3 - ISBN 0-340-76545-3

The Message of a Master
By John McDonald
ISBN 0-931432-95-2

The Celestine Prophecy- An Adventure
By James Redfield
ISBN 0-533-40902-6

Anastasia- The Ringing Cedar series -Book 1
By Vladimir Megre
ISBN 978-0-9801812-0-3

A Course in Miracles
By The Foundation for Inner Peace
ISBN 0-670-86975-9

I AM I The Indweller of Your Heart—Book One

The Winds of Change
By Stephanie J. King
ISBN 9780954242169

The Day my life Changed
By Carmel Reilly
ISBN 978-1-84509-420-1

Confessions of a Pilgrim
Bu Paulo Coelho
ISBN 0-7225-3293-8

A Mind of your Own
By Betty Shine
ISBN 0-00-255894-7

Angel Inspiration
By Diana Cooper
ISBN 0-340-73323-3

Chicken Soup for the Soul
By Jack Canfield and Mark Victor Hansen
ISBN 0-09185-428-8

The Complete Book of Dreams
By Edwin Raphael
ISBN 0-572-01714-6

The Bible Code
By Michael Drosnin
ISBN 0-297-82994-7

Noah Finn & the Art of Suicide
By E.Rachael Hardcastle
ISBN: 978-1999968816

Noah Finn & the Art of Conception
By E. Rachael Hardcastle
ISBN: 978-1999968861

ABOUT THE AUTHOR

David has helped to conduct spiritual development and healing circles for over 25 years. He has also been a guest speaker—sharing his enlightened experiences to promote 'oneness'—at various Mind, Body and Spirit engagements across the UK.

Through inner-dictation, dream interpretation, meditation, mindfulness, pre-cognition, and healing, the books he co-writes with 'Spirit' provide you with the foundation to discover your own path of truth. With a renewed sense of purpose, the spiritual guidance and education you receive can help you reach the goal of self-realization and bliss within the permanence of love and light.

David is tee-total and a vegetarian, who loves the sunshine, nature, animals, and his wife!

INVITATION FROM DAVID KNIGHT

If you enjoyed reading *I AM I The Indweller of Your Heart—Book One*, you can download *Deliverance of Love, Light and Truth* for free when you join David's mission for a 'full and blissful life'.

To learn more, visit www.AscensionForYou.com

Follow us on Facebook@ https://www.facebook.com/AscensionForYou
or Twitter@ https://twitter.com/ascensionforyou

and become part of our community who love to receive uplifting messages for the heart and soul!

I AM I The Indweller of Your Heart—Book One

Want to let others know what you think? Please make your opinion known by leaving a 'star rating' with one-click on Amazon.com or Amazon.co.uk and/or a review at your favourite online retailer.

Thank you!

www.ingramcontent.com/pod-product-compliance
Lightning Source LLC
LaVergne TN
LVHW011830060526
838200LV00053B/3965